DyslexiaLand

DyslexiaLand

A Field Guide for Parents of Children with Dyslexia

Cheri Rae

OLYMPUS PRESS

DyslexiaLand by Cheri Rae
ISBN: 978-0934161-75-6
DyslexiaLand © 2018 Olympus Press, an imprint of
The Trailmaster, Inc.

Book Design by Lisa DeSpain
Cover art and illustrations by Liz Taylor
Published by Olympus Press
This book was typeset in part with the font Dyslexie, designed by Christian Boer

For more information and resources for dyslexia, visit DyslexiaLand.com

Portions of this book have appeared previously in the *Santa Barbara Independent, Santa Barbara Daily Sound*, *Santa Barbara View*, and online at decodingdyslexiaca.org

Comments, conversations, and events shared in this book are from true-life experiences. Some names and identifying characteristics of individuals have been changed to protect their privacy.

For Daniel and the 1 in 5
who change the world with their
keen minds and unique perspectives.

"Start by doing what's necessary,
Then do what's possible; and suddenly you
are doing the impossible."

St. Francis of Assisi

Contents

Education, Who's in Special Education, Who's Not, and Why, Requesting Testing, The IEP Meeting, Tips for the IEP Meeting, Supreme Court Support, Special Education Insider Tips, Parents' Special Education Action Plan, Speaking Their Language: Acronyms in Special Education

9 Advocating for Your Child /

Beware of the "Wait to Fail" Approach, Why Educators Can't and Often Don't Help Dyslexic Students, Become and Advocate, Time is on Their Side. Not Yours, You Won't Believe Your Ears, Going Legal, Burned Up and Burned Out, When Parents Have Dyslexia, Multicultural Dyslexia Awareness, Student Self-Advocacy, Family Matters and Teamwork, Dyslexia Warrior Moms, How to Address the School Board, Parents' Advocacy Plan

10 Dyslexia at Home and in the Community /

Effects on Family Life, Friends and Extended Family, Homework, Details, Details, Details, Extracurricular Activities, Tips for Playtime, What's on the Menu?, Dyslexia as a Public Health Issue, Dyslexia in the Religious Community, Divine Intervention, At Home with Dyslexia

11 What You Need to Know Before You Go /

Costs Associated with Dyslexia, Eight Great Ways to Get Help, The Ten Essentials, The Serenity Prayer

PART III TRAVELING THROUGH THE GRADES

12 Elementary School / 233

Teacher Training, Making Progress, Switching Schools, Retention, Elementary Education for Parents, Hitting the Third Grade Wall, Considering Special Education, Five IEP Tips for Parents, Standardized Testing and Students with Dyslexia, Transition from Elementary to Middle School To-Do List

13 Middle School / 249

Middle School Challenges, Middle School to High School Transition To-Do List, Sample Memo from Parents

14 Dyslexia High / 257

Get Involved and Stay Involved, Be Prepared, When Administrators and Teachers Just Don't Get Dyslexia, Remediation or Accommodation?, Exit Exams and Other Requirements, College Testing, Ten Strategies for High School Success, Reflections: Graduation Day

Foreword

DyslexiaLand is a treasure of a book chock full of insight and concrete tips that will be invaluable for any family of a dyslexic child, or even a dyslexic child.

Author Cheri Rae shifts the paradigm of how we look at dyslexia from the start when she moves us away from thinking of dyslexia as a learning difference instead of a disability. By vividly describing all the pitfalls and aspects of being dyslexic in a country that has not yet embraced the concept of neurodiversity, we are brought into the darker side of DyslexiaLand.

So many parents face the hurdles described here that there will be a constant feeling of recognition; "that is what we face every day." Cheri Rae's commitment to helping children with dyslexia comes through every sentence, and her personal experience as a mother raising her dyslexic son infuses each word with authenticity and heart.

I have navigated the world as a dyslexic myself and then as the mother of a dyslexic daughter. I wish I could say lots has changed in public schools, but the reality is that mainstream schools still have not changed anywhere near enough. Very few families are lucky enough to get their child into one of the enlightened public school programs designed specifically for kids with dyslexia.

Parents are left to contemplate how to afford private tutoring or tuition at a private dyslexia school—effective solutions, but available only to a small percentage of kids who are lucky enough to have access to these opportunities.

Books like this one can help parents learn what is needed to help their child. *DyslexiaLand* covers a lot of ground as it prepares families for the obstacles they will face in today's landscape.

But that is not all you get from reading this gem. After describing the emotional fog that children feel when they encounter a school system that doesn't help them, Cheri Rae makes sure you learn about opportunities and strategies for success as well as the opportunities for all of us to change the system.

This is an inspiring book and should be in easy reach on the bookshelf of every family with a dyslexic child.

—Peggy Stern

Founder, Dyslexiaville

Producer, *The Super d! Show*

Dyslexiaville.com

Introduction

No matter how often I hear them, the stories moms tell me always touch my heart.

Anna and I are seated across the table from each other, sipping coffee. Eyes brimming with tears, in a voice just above a whisper, Anna's words tumble out: "My son is so smart but the teachers say he isn't trying hard enough. I help him at home as much as I can, but he struggles so much, and isn't getting anywhere. What is going to happen to him if he never learns to read?"

It's usually the mothers—confused and exhausted, yet still strong and determined—who seek help for their children with dyslexia.

I offer a tissue, and ask the obvious question: "And how's your son coping with all this?"

"He is beginning to feel dumb and to hate school."

"And you?"

"They keep telling me to read more to him, but I have, ever since he was a baby! Then they say that he is distracted because of ADD, and he needs to be medicated, which I don't want to do. I feel so helpless."

I know her story. I've lived it. And heard similar stories from so many moms — and from dads and grandparents as well.

"What's a mother to do?" she asks.

A parent of a child with dyslexia can do a lot, I will explain later. Particularly when that parent understands how a child with dyslexia learns, and where and how to get help.

Before addressing the learning challenges of their children, though, it's critical that parents recognize the strengths of their children, who shine like bright lights with abilities, and with passions and enthusiasms far beyond their struggles with reading and spelling.

"What does your son love to do?" I ask.

Anna is caught off balance. She looks surprised, then relieved. "Well, he's really into Legos," she says with a slight smile. "Always has been. We've bought him so many sets, and he always puts them together as fast as he gets them. Without looking at the directions. He makes all kinds of complicated towers and contraptions. He's completely focused, and can work on them for hours at a time."

I nod in recognition, "My son is just like that when he builds remote control cars."

"And he loves to swim," she continues. "And play water polo. You can't get him out of the pool."

Introduction

While working as a dyslexia advocate, this dialogue has played out time and time again, one story after another from tearful mothers, who vary substantially by cultural background, profession, financial status, ethnicity, educational level, and even by their ability to speak English. And yet as diverse as they may be as people, as parents attempting to help their children with dyslexia get what they need from a public school system, their experiences are remarkably, indeed dishearteningly, similar: extreme difficulties with getting school officials to give them a straight answer, a timely assessment, or any hope at all that their child is making progress.

Similar, too, are the wrenching descriptions of the experiences their children have in school: the humiliation of trying to read out loud; the embarrassment of being left out of a field trip that rewards accelerated readers; dread of taking a test they know they're going to fail, even though they studied for hours.

Always, in counterpoint, is the array of strengths and interests these otherwise bright children display outside the classroom: Theresa likes to do science experiments at home; Pablo likes to cook. Soccer players, karate kids, bicycle motocross racers, musicians, singers, dancers, actors, those who create extraordinary paintings or who love animals. The sky's the limit for these wonderfully creative, accomplished, and strongly right-brained kids.

This strange juxtaposition of strengths in activities and weaknesses in the classroom clearly reveals that these sharp and spirited children are on the wrong path in school, the place where they spend so much of their time, often with their talents constrained and their spirits crushed.

How do I know? Because I've been there.

I started out as "just" a mom for my daughter and son, a mom who happily volunteered to bake cupcakes, drive on field trips, and make costumes for class plays. But when I tried to get help for my son with dyslexia, I discovered reading programs that didn't work, encountered teachers who knew nothing about dyslexia or how to teach dyslexic students in the way they learn, talked with school psychologists without a clue, and found Special Education especially unhelpful.

By the time my son entered the third grade I had become one of "those moms." I was seen as a problem parent, whose very presence elicited sighs from administrators, defensive comments from Special Ed staff, and wariness from classroom teachers. By the time my son entered the seventh grade and was reading at a second grade level, I was one provoked Mama Bear. I finally found the dyslexia-friendly instruction my son needed at a private learning center and negotiated with the school district to pay for it.

After months of intense instruction at Lindamood-Bell, he was reading (and doing math) at grade level. Yay!

That's how I became a dyslexia advocate—not by choice but by necessity, first working on behalf of my own child, then working as a volunteer to help other children, then "going pro," thanks to a grant from a visionary philanthropist with dyslexia who remembers the painful experience of being branded "mentally retarded" as a child.

Along with my work "in the trenches" with dyslexia, my background as a newspaper columnist gave me a useful perspective on the school system.

During my tenure at the (now defunct) *Daily Sound*, I wrote about politics, and got to know how local government worked. And didn't work. I wrote about City Hall, county government, planning commissions, and boards of review. I covered their bad decisions and bad planning, cost over-runs and cover-ups, the lack of transparency and accountability.

To my dismay, I found that the school district bureaucracy was a lot more like a government bureaucracy than I ever imagined. The difficulties my son and other children with dyslexia were having in school were in a large measure related to a dysfunctional district that refused to take responsibility for educating its dyslexic students—and yet pretended differently.

This realization sometimes made me a stranger in a strange land. There I was—a self-taught mother telling tenured teachers and highly paid, high-level administrators about the 1 in 5 children with dyslexia in their charge, suggesting that despite their lame claims to the contrary and resolute resistance to change, they *could* teach these children in the way they learn.

Advocating for children with dyslexia took place in a world unto itself, a weird world with its own language, politics, culture and traditions. I tried to understand the rules that governed this place — where parents had to fight for services from a rigid bureaucracy that even refused to use the word "dyslexia."

Eventually I had some success as an advocate, helping parents, one at a time, get the services they needed to help their children with dyslexia. But what about all those other sons and daughters, whose parents were not able to make the case? How could I help them, empower them?

As a writer I was stumped: How could I communicate this weird world to parents so that they could advocate for their children on their own?

The answer came to me in an unusual way, in a cosmic moment.

My husband John McKinney (aka The Trailmaster) is the author of 30 books about hiking. He spends a lot of time on the trail researching hikes and talking to hikers. One beautiful morning, he was slinging his pack over a shoulder and heading out the door for a hike and I was preparing papers for a long day of meetings with school administrators. The contrast between the natural world where John was headed and the human-made bureaucracy where I would spend my day overwhelmed me and as we said our goodbyes, I burst out: "Have fun out in the *real* world. I'm stuck here in DyslexiaLand."

The word just popped out. I had never thought it, said it before.

DyslexiaLand.

Suddenly I felt unstuck in time, and flashed back 20 years to another place that touched my heart, captured my attention, and moved me to action. A real place— the eastern Mojave Desert in California, a magnificently scenic land poorly managed, and mistreated by cattle overgrazing, illegal mining operations, and by off-road vehicle races and use that scarred the land and wreaked havoc on the desert tortoise population.

It was a land unknown by the public, and barely known by its federal administrators, by its users and abusers, and even by the conservationists who wanted to preserve it as a national park.

Surely we would make better decisions about what to do with this desert wilderness if we knew more about it, I thought. I resolved to literally and figuratively put this land on the map.

The eastern fringe of the Mojave Desert had colorful names like Zzyzx, Lava Beds, Pyramid Canyon and Rainbow Basin, Fort Piute, and Hole-in-the-Wall, and there sure was a lot of it—1.5 million acres. It was challenging fieldwork, driving slowly along bad dirt roads, hiking up remote canyons and across trackless sand dunes, out there with the roadrunners, chuckwallas and bighorn sheep.

After I spearheaded a map project in collaboration with the U.S. Bureau of Land Management and the Sierra Club, I wrote a guidebook to what we liked to call the "Crown Jewel of the California Desert." The map and guidebook were sent to members of Congress and after much determined effort by conservationists, Congress voted to create Mojave National Preserve, and place it under the protection of the National Park Service.

From "desert wasteland" to national parkland! What a change in perception!

Sunset Magazine praised *Mojave National Preserve: A Visitors Guide* as: "A lively and detailed description of attractions, habitats and issues." I was pleased to play a small part in the preservation of this land and in helping Americans discover its wonders.

It struck me: *If I could map and describe a desert land, I could do the same for DyslexiaLand.*

If I could help people to get to know, travel though, and advocate for a real but unknown land, surely I could help children and their parents journey through DyslexiaLand, an imaginary, yet all too real place with a population of 1 in 5.

My first effort to present DyslexiaLand was as a pocket-sized book with a fold-out map intended as an introduction to the contrasting ways of experiencing dyslexia in school: one of obstacles and stress, the other of opportunities and success. It was a good start, but more was needed.

The concept of "DyslexiaLand" as an alternate reality resonated with parents from Washington to North Carolina, New Mexico to New Jersey, and as far away as Australia. Parents told me their stories: of frustration with school officials, their difficulties getting services, and their fears for their children's futures. This book is much enriched by the stories of these parents, many of whom belong to Decoding Dyslexia, a parent-led movement to increase awareness of dyslexia.

When parents are well-informed about dyslexia, empowered to advocate strongly for their children, and determined to get what they need—and what the law requires—the 13-year-long journey with a child with dyslexia through public school can be a rewarding one. Really!

This guide will help you get to know the land and people of DyslexiaLand, a place with a culture and language all its own. You'll learn the best ways to travel through the grades and how to develop your advocacy skills to secure the education your child deserves.

Keep your moral compass pointing north, keep your sense of humor, keep calm and carry on.

Welcome to DyslexiaLand.

—Cheri Rae
Santa Barbara, CA
DyslexiaLand, USA

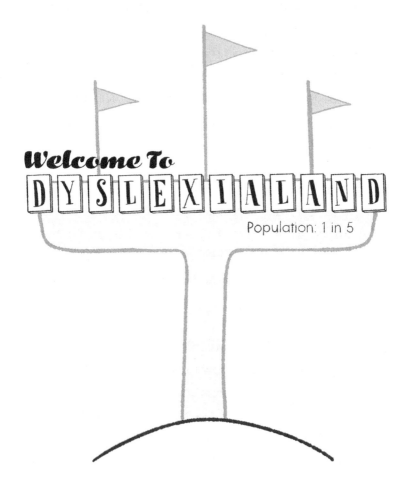

PART I

WELCOME TO DYSLEXIALAND

We've read about Alice in Wonderland and sung about "Toyland, Toyland, Little girl and boy land." Maybe as kids we were lucky enough to go to Disneyland or LegoLand, or have had the opportunity to take our kids to these wonderful places.

Perhaps we've traveled to real lands such as Switzerland or Thailand. Or to real places with imaginative names like the "Land of a Thousand Lakes" (Minnesota) or "Land of Enchantment" (New Mexico).

Who wouldn't want to travel to the proverbial "Land of Plenty" or to the "Land of Milk and Honey"?

When you have a school-aged child with dyslexia—like 1 in 5 parents—you will find yourself, likely to your surprise, traveling through a different sort of territory.

I call it DyslexiaLand.

Although it may be imaginatively named, it's an all-too-real place where children live, learn and play. Millions of parents and their children with dyslexia travel this land. Most do so without preparation, an itinerary, or a guide.

And that's a hard way to go.

Before embarking on a trip to Iceland, Greenland, Swaziland, or any other exotic land, your preparations would likely include acquiring a map, a guidebook, and getting tips from someone who has traveled there before. Such pre-trip planning helps travelers make the most of their journeys and make the best use of their time.

WELCOME TO DYSLEXIALAND

Even travelers to fantasy worlds, such as the mega-theme parks of Disneyworld and Disneyland—use guidebooks to make the most of a trip to the "Happiest Place on Earth."

(By the way, it's no coincidence that creative genius Walt Disney was dyslexic as were/are many of his famed "Imagineers," including architects, artists and animators.)

A landscape of the imagination is what you make of it and your experience is colored by the length of time you spend there. Parents and their children spend a few fun vacation days in Disneyland; parents and their children with dyslexia spend 13 years and about 2,340 not-so-fun school days in DyslexiaLand.

My hope is to make your journey through Dyslexia-Land easier and more rewarding with the help of this field guide and by serving as a tour guide. I successfully led my son with dyslexia from kindergarten through high school, founded The Dyslexia Project and a Parent Resource Center, advocated on behalf of many students with dyslexia, and helped parents get the programs and services their children need.

This field guide will help you understand the arcane laws of the land, interpret the language of fast-talking educators, and lead you through bureaucracies large and small with the goal of getting the most out of public school for your child with dyslexia.

DyslexiaLand is a strange land indeed, where:

✱ 1 in 5 students are not taught in the way they learn.

✱ Dyslexia is the reluctantly mentioned "D" word, referred to confusingly as "Specific Learning Disability," which calls to mind the evil Lord Voldemort in the Harry Potter tales, referred to as "You Know Who" or "He Who Must Not Be Named."

✱ Dyslexia is nearly always treated as a disability and not as a learning difference for children who have unique abilities and strengths.

The land is strange, and the customs, language, and laws of DyslexiaLand are stranger still.

When you enter DyslexiaLand, you find yourself dependent on the kindness of strangers, that is to say the goodwill, experience and expertise of those employed by the public schools to educate our children. You may find kind strangers—teachers who care, Special Ed instructors who go the extra mile, principals determined not to let any student in their charge get left behind.

Or you may find unkind strangers, teachers who don't know about dyslexia and who are defensive about their lack of training, Special Ed instructors who treat students as slow, lazy, and unmotivated, and principals who blame parents for their poorly performing children.

DyslexiaLand is a more pleasant experience for travelers when the strangers are kind and go out of their way to help. But whether these strangers are kind or not, helpful or not, travel through DyslexiaLand is difficult because most public schools are institutionally and systematically dysfunctional when it comes to teaching students with dyslexia.

Teachers, pleasant or not, caring or not, are nearly always poorly trained to recognize dyslexia, or in how to instruct their students who have dyslexia. School officials, polite or not, hard working or not, are mostly uninformed about the kind of instruction needed for these kids and how to supervise the delivery of this instruction.

Parents may spend years trying to figure out the complexity of DyslexiaLand and, while they're learning their lessons, their children with dyslexia are decidedly not learning theirs: how to read, write, spell, do math and deal with a myriad of processing and executive function issues that may accompany their bright, neurodiverse minds.

But parents really don't have that kind of time. And neither do their children.

This guide will save a lot of time and even some money by pinpointing the services your child needs early on and avoiding larger costs—financial and emotional—that your family may incur if your child's school struggles are not identified and addressed in the early grades.

Let's begin by getting to know the land and people of DyslexiaLand.

Walt Disney

Whoopi Goldberg

Henry Winkler

Steve Jobs

Pablo Picasso

Cher

1

Land and People

Early explorers ventured into *Terra Incognita,* The Unknown Territory, without a map. Some were tossed by storms, defeated by the elements and lost forever. Others followed the stars, overcame the elements, and discovered riches and wonders in marvelous places.

So it is for travelers to DyslexiaLand. They cross into a little known territory. It's a journey few imagined they would ever undertake, and most who cross the border into DyslexiaLand are unaware of the land or people, perils or possibilities that await them.

Researchers study dyslexia from Singapore to Sri Lanka, Finland to the Philippines, and students are identified in such far-flung locales as Uganda and South Africa, Brazil and Argentina. Despite, or because of, its universal occurrence, dyslexia poses challenges for children and their parents everywhere.

At the beginning of most of life's journeys, parents lead their children. DyslexiaLand, though, turns this convention upside down; it's the children who lead their parents into this uncharted territory, and parents follow, reacting to the unexpected difficulties navigating in the school environment.

Parents typically bring their children to school, leave them in the hands of teachers, and trust their kids will get a good education. Only after the school repeatedly fails to teach their children to read, do parents begin to realize that something is wrong and they must act.

For parents, the task is to lead their children through the dark and confusing place DyslexiaLand *can* be into the vibrant place of promise and potential DyslexiaLand *should* be.

DyslexiaLand: Land of Contrasts

Approaches to instruction in DyslexiaLand vary widely by geographical area. The Individuals with Disabilities Education Act (IDEA) is a federal law designed to ensure that students with a disability are provided with Free Appropriate Public Education (FAPE) that is tailored to their individual needs. However, it is up to the states and local school districts to interpret this law and to implement programs and provide services to comply with the law.

Every state, indeed nearly every zip code, has a different way of regarding dyslexia and delivering services. Institutional knowledge, socioeconomic factors, and costs are huge determinants in how and how much a school district helps students with dyslexia.

Texas was the first state to pass a dyslexia law in 1985. Since then, each school district has been required to screen and provide treatment for students with dyslexia, and is required to provide appropriate information and intervention. However, having legislation in place is no guarantee of appropriate services in a particular district, and the state's record of actually delivering services to students with dyslexia is spotty.

Mississippi developed a state dyslexia handbook in 2010 and has created a statewide program that offers "technical assistance" to individual schools, school districts, parents and community members. The state also helps parents access information about its dyslexia scholarship program.

California, the most populous state and so often an example of progressive leadership, lags behind. Even after the passage of recent legislation, the Golden State does not require testing to identify students with dyslexia. Additionally, the state lacks standards for the training of teachers in how to instruct students with dyslexia.

Within each state, the city, county, and regional school districts, as well as schools within a district, develop reputations (positive and negative) for how they teach (or don't teach) students with dyslexia and especially how they implement Special Education services.

If and how students are taught, and even if and how services are given, depends a great deal on the vision and leadership of a particular district's top administration, as well as the willingness of teaching staff to implement programs and services.

District policies can change quickly, depending on the interests and abilities of the leadership. Federal, state and regional politics play a big part in the way the challenges of dyslexia are addressed and how the funding is allocated to programs that serve students with dyslexia. (*See "Politics" discussion in this guide*)

The Deserts of DyslexiaLand

Drive across one of the great deserts of the American Southwest and you'll encounter signs that read: "Next Services 100 Miles." It can be scary to keep going, not knowing what lies ahead. Your journey through DyslexiaLand can be like that, since much of it seems like a vast desert without services for children with dyslexia for miles around.

Families who live in dyslexia deserts—in school districts that fail to provide an appropriate education for dyslexic students—may feel like they're stranded in barren terrain with no services in sight. In such a situation, parents may be forced to search for—and even travel great distances—to obtain services for their children.

With lots of effort, and a bit of luck, parents will find outposts that provide the needed services: dyslexia-oriented community reading centers, a university, or a hospital; qualified tutors or educational therapists in private practice; a true Orton-Gillingham oasis in a private school designed to meet the needs of dyslexic students. The cost of these services can be high, and can vary greatly depending upon location and region.

Forbidding the dyslexia desert may be, but it must be crossed with courage and conviction. When considering their options, parents must remember that the worst option of all is to wait, stay stuck in a barren land, and think that the situation will get better without taking action and leading their children to a better place.

Dyslexia Around the World

As a biological, neurological difference in the brain, dyslexia exists everywhere.

The United Nations Educational, Scientific and Cultural Organization (UNESCO) has long recognized the need to raise awareness and provide information about dyslexia among its member nations and non-governmental organizations. Since 2010, when it commissioned reports in its six languages (Arabic, Chinese, English, French, Russian and Spanish), UNESCO has teamed with Dyslexia International to convene World Dyslexia Forums. These forums address scientific discoveries and research, good teaching practices and the use of information and communication technologies around the globe.

Dyslexia International provides free online, interactive training in dyslexia teaching practices in several languages in partnership with Massive Open Online

Courses (mooc.org). Dedicated to "supporting children with difficulties in reading and writing," the organization offers a wealth of information for parents and teachers on its website (dyslexia-international.org).

English, with its 26 letters and 44 different sounds, is challenging enough for individuals with dyslexia; imagine having to learn some 3000 different characters in Chinese that represent meanings rather than sounds.

In the forthright manner it addresses dyslexia, Great Britain leads the way for English-speaking countries around the world. Educators have been working for greater awareness and opportunity for students with dyslexia for many years. The notion of "dyslexia-friendly schools" and a "dyslexia-friendly society" have made dyslexia a commonly accepted learning difference that is accommodated in schools and beyond throughout the nation.

Britain may have more openness and awareness about dyslexia because many members of the Royal Family have dyslexia, including Prince Harry and Princess Beatrice, as well as James Middleton, brother of Catherine, Duchess of Cambridge.

British schools are required to provide early assessment and intervention, and to teach and support students with dyslexia. The nation's Department for Education has developed an Inclusion Development Programme as part of "the government's strategy to improve outcomes for children with special educational needs."

Dyslexia in the workplace is a commonly addressed issue in Britain, unlike in the United States. A government report revealed that within the country's top eaves-dropping agency, code-breakers and cryptographists typically have dyslexia, an asset in their ability to see codes, with their patterns, repetitions and omissions.

The Greek public school system has made great strides with early identification in the last 20 years by adapting Britain's approach and by recognizing in the early grades that 1 in 5 students have dyslexia. At the secondary level, written exams are replaced by oral exams for students with dyslexia. These students may even take final exams, and the Panhellenic General Examinations ("the Greek SAT") orally.

The People of DyslexiaLand

Dyslexia occurs in 20 percent of the population. That makes it more common than people with blue eyes (17 percent), people who are left-handed (10 percent), people who are gay (4 percent). In other words, dyslexia is about as common as individuals who read e-books, consider themselves highly sensitive, or have a tattoo.

A vast majority of the public is unaware of the high percentage of people with dyslexia, and the charac-teristics of dyslexia. Many believe dyslexics see things backwards, and aren't very smart because they read poorly and can't spell. Only a fraction of the public believes that there are any positive attributes of dyslexia.

Even though dyslexia is so prevalent it is generally not known that people who are dyslexic live full, happy and productive lives. This misunderstanding suggests that the dyslexia community has a lot of work to do in order to educate the public.

A famous dyslexic who wants to put an end to this misunderstanding is billionaire entrepreneur Richard Branson, of Virgin Enterprises. In 2017, he announced the formation of a new global charity, Made by Dyslexia (*madebydyslexia.org*), "to help the world properly understand and support dyslexia." In launching his organization, Branson reported the findings of recent research that includes perceptions of dyslexia: just 4 percent of the population views dyslexia as a positive trait, and only 19 percent think that dyslexia enables creativity. That stands in contrast to the reports by individuals who actually have dyslexia: 84 percent believe they have higher than average creative skills.

Clearly, a major gap lies between what is known and what is believed about dyslexia! However, that gap is narrowing as dyslexia emerges from the shadows into the spotlight, and more individuals—famous and not famous—share their stories, experiences, and insights.

Luminaries of DyslexiaLand

A short list of individuals who shine a light in DyslexiaLand.

Researchers

Dr. Fernette Eide and Dr. Brock Eide, founders of the nonprofit, website, and book, *The Dyslexic Advantage*. The mission of Dyslexic Advantage is to promote the positive identity, community, and achievement of dyslexic people by focusing on their strengths." dyslexicadvantage.org

Dr. Fumiko Hoeft, Associate Professor of Child & Adolescent Psychiatry and Director of BrainLENS at UCSF. As a psychiatrist and developmental cognitive neuroscientist, she uses neuroimaging techniques to understand how the brain develops and functions in those with dyslexia. brainlens.org

Dr. Louisa Moats, a prolific author who has consulted on a number of national studies to improve literacy interventions. She was the project director of the National Institute of Child Health and Human Development (NICHD) Early Interventions Project, and is an internationally recognized authority on teacher training. Read her classic piece, "Teaching Reading is Rocket Science."

Dr. Guinevere Eden, Director of the Center for the Study of Learning at Georgetown University Medical Center. She was among the first to study brain imaging with the fMRI and dyslexia in 1996, and continues her important research. "Dyslexia may be common," she has noted, "but there is nothing simple about it." She has testified before the U.S. Senate on the need to bridge the gap between science and education.

Dr. Mark Seidenberg, cognitive neuro-scientist at the University of Wisconsin, Madison, author of *Language at the Speed of Sight: How We Read, Why So Many Can't, and What Can Be Done About It*. He focuses on the disconnect between the science of reading and classroom practices.

Dr. Sally Shaywitz and Dr. Bennett Shaywitz, Yale Center of Dyslexia and Creativity, authors of *Overcoming Dyslexia*. They originated the notion of dyslexia as a "Sea of Strengths" that include creativity and higher order critical thinking. dyslexia.yale.edu

Dr. Maryanne Wolf, author of *Proust and the Squid: The story and science of the reading brain,* and *Tales of Literacy for the 21st Century*. She serves as the director of Tufts University's Center for Reading and Language Research.

Advocates

Dean Bragonier, advocate who swam around Martha's Vineyard to raise awareness about dyslexia, contending: "A dyslexic who goes to school every day has far more courage than someone who gets in the water with sharks." His organization, NoticeAbility, creates curriculum dedicated to building strengths of dyslexic students in engineering, entrepreneurialism, art and architecture. noticeability.org

Richard LaVoie, former headmaster, now a consultant about learning differences, author of *It's So Much Work to Be Your Friend: Helping the Child with Learning Disabilities Find Social Success*. He is an enthusiastic lecturer and his F.A.T. City workshop is a classic (view it on YouTube). ricklavoie.com

John Rodrigues, author of the autobiographical *High School Dropout to Harvard: My Life with Dyslexia*. He grew up with unrecognized dyslexia, dropped out of high school in his junior year, and made his way around the world as a ice sculptor on cruise ships. Today he is a college graduate, educator and dyslexia advocate. Thinklexic.org.

Jonathan Mooney, author of *Learning Outside the Lines* and *The Short Bus*. He is an advocate for dyslexia and ADD/ADHD and co-founder (along with author David Flink and other then-students at Brown University) of Project Eye-to-Eye, a mentoring program for youth with learning differences. jonathanmooney.com

Ben Foss, inventor of the Intel Reader, author of *The Dyslexia Empowerment Plan: A Blueprint for Renewing your Child's Confidence and Love of Learning*, and founder of Headstrong Nation. His mission is to "empower adult dyslexics to own their dyslexia, understand it, and to develop new ways of learning and working based on their individual profiles." headstrongnation.org

Filmmakers

Harvey Hubbell, Emmy-award-winning filmmaker who created "Dislecksia, The Movie," a funny and thought-provoking documentary about dyslexia. It includes Hubbell's own story, man-on-the-street-interviews, leading researchers, and interviews with famous individuals with dyslexia.

James Redford, writer and director of "The Big Picture: Rethinking Dyslexia," which documents the strengths and struggles of Redford's own son, Dylan, as he prepared for college. The film includes interviews with researchers, accomplished individuals with dyslexia and features Dr. Sally Shaywitz. His wife **Kyle Redford**, a teacher, has authored numerous articles about dyslexia.

Stephen and Jennifer Polk, director-producers of "School Stories: Divided States of Dyslexia**.**" They have traveled across the country and met with individuals with dyslexia, parents, educators, and administrators to produce a series of first-person videos. identifying.org

Peggy Stern, founder of Dyslexiaville and creative force behind *The Super d! Show*, a web-based series of shows starring children with dyslexia or ADHD. The Oscar-winning documentary filmmaker graduated from Harvard, and draws on her experiences growing up dyslexic and advocating for her dyslexic daughter. Dyslexiaville.com

Other Influencers

Susan Barton, Bright Solutions for Dyslexia, her site includes many videos and helpful suggestions about identifying and accommodating dyslexia, plus her reading program that teaches parents to teach their children how to read. bartonreading.com

Dr. Kelli Sandman-Hurley and **Tracy Block Zaretsky,** Dyslexia Training Institute, offer presentations, online courses and a "Dyslexia for a Day" simulation. Dyslexiatraininginstitute.org

Dr. Michael Hart, child psychologist, has decades of experience in addressing dyslexia. He offers great resources on his site. doctormichaelhart.com

Jamie Martin, dyslexia Assistive Technology expert. atdyslexia.com

Barbara and Ed Wilson, co-founders of Wilson Language Training, and Orton-Gillingham-based approach to reading. It is widely used in in libraries, reading centers and enlightened school districts. They also offer professional learning opportunities for educators. wilsonlanguage.com

Podcasters

The Codpast: "Fresh Content for Students and Adults with Dyslexia," insightful interviews from the United Kingdom.

Dyslexia is Our Superpower Podcast, by Gibby Booth, focuses on the positive aspects of dyslexia, how to find and unlock each person's strengths.

Dyslexic and Unstoppable, hosted by Douglas Curtiss and Lucie Curtiss. Providing tools and strategies to help dyslexic children rediscover their inner power.

The Dyslexia Quest with Elishiva Schwartz, neurodiversity advocate on a quest to decode the power of the dyslexic mind in a series of interviews with prominent individuals with dyslexia.

Famous People with Dyslexia

A short list of accomplished role models in DyslexiaLand.

Actors and Entertainers: Jennifer Aniston. Cher. Jewel. Usher. Orlando Bloom. Tom Cruise. Whoopi Goldberg. Salma Hayek. Eddie Izzard. Keira Knightly. John Lennon. Jay Leno. George Lopez. Jack Nicholson. Edward James Olmos. Ozzy Osbourne. Carly Simon. Will Smith. Octavia Spencer. Joss Stone. Channing Tatum. Bella Thorne. Robin Williams. Henry Winkler.

Architects: Hugh Newell Jacobsen. Richard Rogers. Takanao Todo. Jorn Utzon.

Athletes: Muhammad Ali. Kami Craig. Meryl Davis. Magic Johnson. Greg Louganis. Pete Rose. Nolan Ryan. Babe Ruth. Jackie Stewart. Tim Tebow.

Artists and Designers: Ansel Adams. Ignacio Gomez. Tommy Hilfiger. Pablo Picasso. Robert Rauschenberg. Auguste Rodin. Vincent Van Gogh. Andy Warhol.

Attorneys: David Boies. Peter Wright.

Authors and Poets: Avi. Agatha Christie. Fannie Flagg. Gustave Flaubert. Thom Hartmann. Ernest Hemingway. John Irving. Debbie Macomber. Dan Pilkey. Edgar Allan Poe. Patricia Polacco. William Butler Yeats. Jules Verne. Victor Villasenor.

Entrepreneurs: Sir Richard Branson. Ingvar Kamprad. Craig McCaw. Jaime Oliver. Paul Orfalea. Jonah Peretti. Anita Roddick. Charles Schwab. Ted Turner. *Shark Tank's* Barbara Corcoran, Daymond John and Kevin O'Leary.

Filmmakers: Walt Disney. Brian Grazer. George Lucas. Steven Spielberg. Quentin Tarantino.

Inventors and Scientists: Maggie Aderin-Pocock. Anne Bancroft. Leonardo da Vinci. Thomas Edison. Michael Faraday. Henry Ford. Galileo Galilei. Bill Gates. Reyn Guyer. William Hewlett. Jack Horner. Dean Kamen. Nicholas Negroponte. Sir Isaac Newton. Evan Paul. Alexander Graham Bell. Steve Jobs. Dean Kamen. Louis Pasteur. Nicolai Tesla. Alan Turing. Eli Whitney. Orville and Wilbur Wright.

Journalists: Erin Brockovich. Gareth Cook. Anderson Cooper. Richard Engel.

Nobel Prize Winners: Winston Churchill. Dr. Baruj Benacerraf. Pierre Curie. Jacques Dubochet. Albert Einstein. Dr. Carol Greider.

Pulitzer Prize Winners: Richard Ford. Philip Schultz. Wendy Wasserstein. Roger Wilkens. E. O. Wilson.

Political Figures: Colorado Senator Michael Bennet. James Carville. Dwight D. Eisenhower. Benjamin Franklin. Colorado Governor John Hickenlooper. New Jersey Governor Thomas Kern. Connecticut Governor Dan Malloy. First Lady of Iceland Dorrit Moussaleff. California Governor Gavin Newsom. Lyndon Johnson. John F. Kennedy. Vermont Governor Pete Shumlin. Woodrow Wilson. Nelson Rockefeller. Eleanor Roosevelt. Erna Solberg, Prime Minister of Norway. Lee Kuan Yew, Prime Minister of Singapore.

Royalty: King Carl XVI Gustav of Sweden. Princess Beatrice. Prince Charles. Prince Harry.

AND....fully 20 percent of the population, and some of the smartest, most creative people who ever lived!

The D-Word

2

Language and Culture

Emily has dyslexia.

Emily is a dyslexic.

Emily is dyslexic.

Emily is a person with dyslexia.

Does it make any difference how we refer to people with dyslexia?

Writers, many dyslexia advocates and those who prefer "person centered language" refer to a person *with dyslexia* rather than *a dyslexic*. Speaking of someone who *has dyslexia* separates the person and the issue, while the phrase *is a dyslexic* identifies the person *as* the issue.

Many individuals who have dyslexia, though, find a sense of ownership, definition and clarity in referring to themselves as dyslexic or a dyslexic. And they point out that saying someone "has dyslexia" defines it as a condition or even a disease—which it certainly is not!

While it's more common to refer to "a person with dyslexia" or "students with dyslexia" rather than as "a dyslexic" or "dyslexics," the differences in phraseology are meant to be respectful, not dismissive in any way. As in any communication, though, parties should address the terminology and decide what works.

However we respectfully refer to individuals with dyslexia, I hope that one day soon the phrases, "He suffers from dyslexia" or "She struggles with dyslexia" are recognized as completely inappropriate and eliminated completely from acceptable vocabulary. Let's replace them with the more positive approaches that recognize dyslexic strengths, something like "blessed with dyslexia" and "successful due to dyslexia."

The term "neurodiversity" is sometimes applied to the complex array of issues associated with dyslexia, and may someday come into wider use, both as a less negative and more accurate description.

The "D" Word

"Dyslexia," from the Greek, means "trouble with words." How ironic that a word that describes difficulty with words is so difficult to understand and to spell!

It's not trouble with words *per se*, it's trouble with reading, writing and spelling them that's challenging for individuals with dyslexia. The trouble comes from difficulty decoding the symbols and understanding the sounds they make, as well as remembering contrary rules about how to spell them.

The journey through DyslexiaLand is made more difficult because of a language barrier—that is to say, the absence of a universally accepted definition of dyslexia, and widespread institutional resistance to using the word "dyslexia." (The reasons for this resistance—economic, political, bureaucratic—are explored elsewhere in this field guide.)

If the definition and use of the word "dyslexia" was a matter of semantics, like the difference between referring to someone as "having dyslexia" or "dyslexic," it would make little difference to the traveler through DyslexiaLand.

However, the way dyslexia is defined and how the word is used (and *not* used) matters a great deal for parents and children on their journey.

Dyslexia Defined

The commonly accepted and prevailing definition of dyslexia is disability-based and focuses solely on the struggles and challenges associated with it.

This definition of dyslexia, from the International Dyslexia Association, is used by the National Institute of Child Health and Human Development (NICHD), and has been adopted by several states in their dyslexia legislation:

"Dyslexia is a specific learning disability that is neurobiological in origin. It is characterized by difficulties with accurate and/or fluent word recognition and by poor spelling and decoding abilities. These difficulties typically result from a deficit in the phonological component of language that is often unexpected in relation to other cognitive abilities and the provision of effective classroom instruction. Secondary consequences may include problems in reading comprehension and reduced reading experience that can impede growth of vocabulary and background knowledge."

The IDEA definition of "specific learning disability" is: "a disorder in one or more of the basic psychological processes involved in understanding or in using language, spoken or written, that may manifest itself in the imperfect ability to listen, think, speak, read, write, spell, or to do mathematical calculations, including conditions such as perceptual disabilities, brain injury, minimal brain dysfunction, dyslexia, and developmental aphasia."

Remember that under the Individuals with Disabilities Act (IDEA), this definition of dyslexia (under the category of specific learning disability) is accepted in Special Education.

Dyslexia advocates suggest changing the dialogue by defining dyslexia for its strengths and its positive attributes. I strongly support this, and came up with:

"Dyslexia is a specific learning ability, neurobiological in origin. It is typically characterized by strengths that may include creative expression, athletic performance, and scientific discovery. The individual with dyslexia often exhibits strengths in big-picture concepts, thinking outside the box, making unexpected connections, and demonstrates an intuitive sense of understanding of people and navigating the natural world. Secondary strengths include a unique learning style that may be visual, auditory, or kinesthetic, the ability to demonstrate knowledge other than with the written word, and a canny sense of entrepreneurialism that may lead to great innovations and financial success."

The British Dyslexia Association uses a definition that includes *both* strengths and challenges, and begins: "A combination of abilities and difficulties which affect the learning process in one or more of reading, spelling and writing."

The DSM-5, published by the American Psychiatric Association is used widely by mental health-care professionals. Some educators are fond of asserting that the Diagnostic and Statistical Manual of Mental Disorders-5 (5th edition) does not include dyslexia. They are wrong.

In the update of 2013, the DSM-5 addresses dyslexia in the category of Specific Learning Disorder:

1. Specific learning disorder with impairment in reading includes possible deficits in:
    * Word reading accuracy
    * Reading rate or fluency
    * Reading comprehension

DSM-5 diagnostic code 315.00.

Note: Dyslexia is an alternative term used to refer to a pattern of learning difficulties characterized by problems with accurate or fluent word recognition, poor decoding, and poor spelling abilities.

A majority of educators use the term "Specific Learning Disorder" or, more frequently, "Specific Learning Disability" instead of "dyslexia." This umbrella term (that no one has ever heard of except in a school setting) causes no end of confusion for parents, and no end of frustration when they finally figure out their child has dyslexia.

The day may come when the neurodiversity characteristics of dyslexia are recognized primarily as a different way of thinking that allows brilliance to emerge — outside of the traditional educational/political/cultural/institutional insistence that defines it as a disability.

The D-word debate is so intense that no less than the US Department of Education felt compelled to weigh in, and in 2015, its Office of Special Education and Rehabilitative Services sent out a "Dear Colleague" letter reaffirming that, indeed, it is okay to say "dyslexia" in our nation's public schools.

The Other "D" Word: Disability

Although the term "learning disability" is applied to students who display characteristics of dyslexia in most school districts in the U.S., many parents and professionals in DyslexiaLand refuse to use it, since most of these students are not disabled in any way; they simply have difficulty performing the tasks required of them in school in the specified manner, and in the time allotted.

Rather than defining individual students as disabled because they do not fit into a system that fails to teach them in the way they learn, parents counter with the suggestion that the situation might be more accurately termed "schooling disability," "teaching disability," or even "dys-teachia," shifting the responsibility back where it belongs, on the institutions and bureaucracies charged with teaching all students.

The term "learning difference" instead of "learning disability" is a more respectful and appropriate way to refer to students with dyslexia, who are not considered disabled anywhere else except in the public school. (However, please do note that in order for students to receive Special Education services and accommodations for dyslexia under federal and state law, they will be classified with a disability—all the way through the system from kindergarten to high school and beyond.)

The "disability" label follows students into higher education. Those college students with dyslexia who choose to obtain accommodations will have to independently seek services from offices named "Disability Resource Center," "Services for Students with Disabilities," or "Disability Support and Services." In a more positive direction the trend in naming such centers is moving toward "Learning Opportunities Program" or "Alternative Learning Center." Three cheers for the University of Southern California and its well-named "Center for Learning and Creativity."

Dyslexia: The Greeks Have Word(s) for It

ΔΥΣΛΕΞΙΑΣ (DYSLEXIA) It's all Greek to me.

My Greek-American friends suggested positive Greek words that could be affixed to individuals with characteristics of dyslexia if we want to acknowledge their gifts and emphasize their potential:

* **Eunoia**: *beautiful thinking*
* **Kairos**: *the perfect, delicate, crucial moment; the fleeting rightness of time; and the place that creates the opportune atmosphere for action, words or movement*
* **Kefi**: *the spirit of joy, enthusiasm, high spirits*
* **Meraki**: *to do something with soul, creativity, or love; to put something of yourself into your work*
* **Eudaimonia:** *human flourishing; contented state of being happy and healthy and prosperous*

What if we taught children and young adults with dyslexia in the way they learned, helped them on the way to their full potential, and could say of them: "Oh, yes, these students have (choose one or more) *eunoia / kairos / kefi / meraki / eudaimonia*; they are so great!"

Dyslexia in Popular Culture

Knowledge about dyslexia has not simply been hidden away in the halls of academia; it has also been the subject of many articles in the popular press for decades.

In 1966, educator Careth Ellingson wrote an article, "Teaching the Dyslexic Child," that was published in the *Saturday Review*.

She stated, "It would be difficult, if not impossible, to find any other disability affecting so many millions of children in the United States today, on which so much research has been done, so many thousands of articles written, and yet which so very little information concerning has reached the average teacher or physician to say nothing of parents and the public. These children are as handicapped by the ignorance surrounding their problem as they are by the problem itself."

In 1972, *Life* Magazine published a story titled "An Agony of Learning," which detailed how students with dyslexia struggle in school. It concluded "The biggest problem facing a child who is diagnosed as learning disabled is getting proper teaching. The greatest handicap for learning disabled children of any age, however, remains ignorance—on the part of pediatricians, teachers, administrators and parents."

A 2002 cover story of *Fortune 500* featured a youthful Charles Schwab on the cover, with the tag line, "The Dyslexic CEO: Charles Schwab, Richard Branson, Craig McCaw and John Chambers triumphed over America's No. 1 learning disorder. Your kid can too." Written by Betsy Morris, it's a groundbreaking piece revealing the link between school struggles experienced by very bright entrepreneurs and their eventual success in business—due to their dyslexic strengths.

Since then, *Time, Newsweek, Wired, Scientific American, The New Yorker,* and many other major publications have published stories about dyslexia. More recently, high circulation magazines published by "big-box" stores have focused on dyslexia. In 2017, dyslexia was featured in the August editions of both the Costco *Connection* magazine and the *Sam's Club* magazine, the latter featuring an article by longtime researcher and advocate of appropriate teacher training, Dr. Louisa Moats.

Dyslexia themes have been a part of television for decades: There was even an ABC Afterschool Special produced in 1984, starring the late River Phoenix and co-starring his younger brother Joaquin (then known as Leaf). "Backward: The Riddle of Dyslexia," is the story of an increasingly troubled junior high student whose dyslexia is finally recognized by a kindly teacher. And in 1992, a made-for-television movie, "The Secret," starred Kirk Douglas as a grandfather with dyslexia who realized his grandson shared the issue with him.

Dyslexia was a recurring theme in "The George Lopez Show," with both father and son dealing with it. Actress Bella Thorne, who has dyslexia, played the character CeCe Jones—also dyslexic—in the Disney show, 'Shake it Up." In one episode, she tearfully explains to her friend Rocky Blue (played by Zendaya) why she has kept her dyslexia a secret.

Many other TV series and movies have featured dyslexic characters, including Ben Affleck's portrayal of Rafe McCawley in "Pearl Harbor," and Cameron Diaz as Maggie in "In Her Shoes." And a couple of dramatic dyslexia themed-movies—both about boys struggling in school until their teachers recognize the cause—include "bAd" and "Like Stars on Earth" (originally released in India as "Taare Zameen Par").

Nowadays, dyslexia is all over the internet, with countless websites and blogs, webinars and podcasts, as well as social media sites and You Tube videos. The availability of so much information, resources, ideas, strategies, even instruction, as well as the ability for individuals to communicate beyond state and national boundaries is of enormous help to parents, and enhances their ability to obtain appropriate services for their children with dyslexia.

Culture of Denial

Few conspiracy theorists are to be found in Dyslexia-Land, though many parents and professionals speculate about why there is a collective denial of dyslexia at every level in academia.

When a parent brings up the possibility that their child may have dyslexia, the notion may be ridiculed, and the issue denied by school officials, even in the face of no improvement in a student's reading, writing and spelling over months and even years.

Here are remarks from dyslexia-denying school psychologists from my collection:

"Dyslexia is a medical issue; if you want to discuss it, go see your pediatrician."

"No, it's not dyslexia. Your child just needs to get more focused and motivated."

"I know about learning disabilities, and this isn't one. And I have a Ph.D."

"Why is it so important for you to call it dyslexia? You stigmatize your child that way."

What Researchers Say

The positive attributes of dyslexia and the high potential of people with dyslexia is evident from research studies. However, school psychologists, teachers, and administrators haven't caught up with the latest science about dyslexia, or brought it into the classroom.

Dr. Fumiko Hoeft, a researcher at the UCSF Dyslexia Center has suggested that dyslexia can even be an "evolutionary advantage." "Dyslexia would have died out over time if it was all bad," she contends.

Dr. Maryanne Wolf of Tufts University asserts: "The single most important implication of research in dyslexia is not ensuring that we don't derail the development of a future Leonardo or Edison; it is making sure that we do not miss the potential of any child. Not all children with dyslexia have extraordinary talents, but every one of them has a unique potential that all too often goes unrealized because we don't know how to tap it."

Dr. Sally Shaywitz of the Yale Center for Dyslexia and Creativity describes dyslexia as an "island of weakness surrounded by a sea of strengths." She explains that the island is decoding, while the sea of strengths includes the skills of reasoning, concept formation, comprehension, general knowledge, problem solving, vocabulary and critical thinking.

Dr. Louisa Moats, nationally renowned teacher, psychologist, and author explains: "If evidence is going to drive our thinking, then all indicators point to this: screen the kids early; teach all the kids who are at risk, skillfully and intensively; and maintain the effort for as long as it takes. Meanwhile, nurture the students' interests, aptitudes, and coping strategies and trust that most are going to make it in real life."

Dr. Brock Eide, who wrote *The Dyslexic Advantage* along with his wife, Dr. Fernette Eide, notes," One of the most important things is to remember to focus on identifying and building strengths. Too often all the focus is on 'fixing what's wrong' rather than celebrating and nurturing what's right, and that's a big mistake. But when it does comes to improving performance in areas of struggle, help should be allocated to the specific child."

Lexiana

Goddess of Dyslexialand

3

Mythology, History, Politics

DyslexiaLand is filled with myths—a few bright tales and more than a few dark ones. The dark myths require our study because they are not grand legends that illustrate the human struggle, but harmful fictions passed along as facts.

But first, a few positive myths from DyslexiaLand.

Author Rick Riordan was inspired to create positive role models for his young dyslexic son—who loved the Greek myths—and conjured a whole new world of demigods and adventures in his *Percy Jackson and the Olympians* series of books. Hero Percy Jackson is a boy who has dyslexia and ADHD, and prevails in part by using strengths he has from his dyslexia. Many of the novels have been turned into movies.

Lexiana, Goddess of DyslexiaLand

Lexiana has come to me out of the mist, while clashing with educators in the Battle for Children with Dyslexia.

Likely this goddess comes to me out of my imagination. And yet *she seems so real*. Maybe, just maybe, she will come to you, too.

Lexiana, warrior goddess of DyslexiaLand, is an inspiration for the warrior moms who fight for their children to get them the education they deserve. A fiercely powerful deity she is, and a striking figure who carries a lamp of enlightenment in one hand, a scroll of wisdom in the other. Lexiana wears a multi-layered gown of many colors, embroidered with pearls of wisdom and golden letters, with a vest of armor to ward off the slings and arrows that come her way. On her feet are sturdy sandals for traversing rocky roads and rough terrain; around her head is a gold halo that glows with the Roman numerals that read: **I in V**.

Like every goddess, Lexiana has her flaws and vulnerabilities. One blind spot is her unshakeable belief (sometimes characterized as naïve) that in speaking truth to power, the truth will always win. She thinks she's indefatigable, though even a goddess gets battle weary, and can only fight for so long.

She stands steadfastly for the protection of children, and is blessed with the qualities of truth, courage, compassion, and a laser-like ability to cut through fog and smoke screens. Lexiana knows the struggle is daunting, and has been known to appear to moms (and occasionally dads), in the most desperate of times, and to channel her wisdom, as well her gentle—and not-so-gentle—powers of persuasion.

Above all, Lexiana inspires, and lives in the hearts and minds of so many mothers who emulate her warrior spirit every single day—and never give up.

Dyslexia and Denial

Denial is a river with a powerful current in DyslexiaLand.

Like climate change deniers, dyslexia deniers are fewer and fewer these days in the face of overwhelming scientific evidence to the contrary. Nevertheless, decade after decade, dyslexia deniers keep coming up with their own research studies, crackpot theories and "experts" who claim that there's *no such thing as dyslexia*. More of the media and education establishment believe and repeat this myth than you might imagine.

By definition, denial is the refusal to accept reality or fact, acting as if that fact or reality does not exist. Psychologists consider denial one of the most primitive of defense mechanisms because it is characteristic of early childhood development. When the discussion turns to dyslexia and early childhood development, it's particularly ironic to find high-level educators in denial about dyslexia.

The earth is flat, Bigfoot is real, and there's no such thing as dyslexia. People cling to these beliefs. DyslexiaLand is populated with a sizeable number of dyslexia-deniers, and you are likely to encounter one, or even many in person, and learn about them online.

In 1992, Dr. Samuel Blumenthal wrote an essay, "Creating Dyslexia: It's as Easy as Pie." In it, he blamed dyslexia on the practice of having students memorize sight words, citing Pavlov's experiments on conditioned response.

In 2009, a Member of Parliament in Britain, Graham Stringer, received a great deal of attention, indeed wrath, for declaring that dyslexia is a "cruel fiction." Stringer asserted that it had been invented by the education establishment to cover up for poor teaching methods.

In 2016, the International Literacy Association, a global advocacy group, raised the ire of dyslexia advocates worldwide when it questioned the very word dyslexia and suggested teachers need not waste their time on the subject.

The ILA declared, "ILA's position is that teachers do not need to spend substantial amounts of time learning about dyslexia, which as has been argued, is a construct of questionable utility."

Of course the International Dyslexia Association, on behalf of students with dyslexia, strongly disagreed with the International Literacy Association.

When an organization like the International Literacy Association dismisses dyslexia, the problems can go from global to local. In my school district, an educator cited the ILA position as a reason to thwart a plan to adopt an Orton-Gillingham reading approach for students with dyslexia. She insisted instead on the balanced literacy approach, a methodology that is not effective for students with dyslexia. This caused a very time-consuming debate that derailed plans, confused other educators, and left students with dyslexia without a reading program that teaches them in the way they learn.

MythLexia: Ten Myths (and Truths) About Dyslexia

MYTH 1: Dyslexia makes you see things backwards

TRUTH: People with dyslexia do not see things backwards, but may have trouble matching letters with the sounds they make. They may confuse several letters, which are the same symbol, just pointed in a different direction, such as b and d; p and q; m and w, u and n.

MYTH 2: Dyslexia is just an excuse for people who aren't motivated or who just aren't very smart.

TRUTH: Individuals with dyslexia often work much harder than those who do not have it, but at some point they may just give up. Dyslexia has no relationship to intelligence. It is often characteristic of individuals who have unique ways of looking at the world, and abilities to be creative problem-solvers.

MYTH 3: Dyslexia is something that you grow out of.

TRUTH: Individuals with dyslexia can learn to compensate and work around it, but the neurological difference is a lifelong characteristic of a unique brain.

MYTH 4: Dyslexia affects more boys than girls.

TRUTH: According to the most current research, dyslexia occurs equally in both genders. Dyslexia may *appear* to occur more often in boys than in girls because of the differences in how the genders deal with it: boys may tend to act out, become the class clown, or act like they don't care about reading or school. Girls may tend to work harder to compensate, trying to please, struggling quietly and getting lost in their schoolwork before indicating they need help. When boys are disruptive and exhibit behavior issues, school officials take a closer look at them, and may discover their dyslexia.

MYTH 5: Dyslexia means reading is impossible.

TRUTH: Individuals with dyslexia can learn to read; however they must be taught with a multisensory structured language approach such as Orton-Gillingham.

MYTH 6: Dyslexia cannot be detected before a student reaches school age.

TRUTH: Dyslexia can be detected in children before they are in kindergarten, if screened appropriately. These early signs indicate they will become struggling readers: inability to rhyme; difficulty sounding out letters and blends; problems remembering the alphabet, days of the week, how to spell their names. Most school districts do not screen students for dyslexia, and operate on a "wait to fail" model, offering interventions only after a student falls far below grade level.

MYTH 7: Dyslexia is rare.

TRUTH: Current research, based in neuroscience, reveals that 1 in 5 individuals may have dyslexia, manifested on a continuum from mild to severe.

MYTH 8: Dyslexia is well-understood by educators.

TRUTH: Teachers rarely receive appropriate training necessary to identify dyslexia in students or how to teach them in the way they learn. It's not uncommon to encounter mid-level and top administrators who lack functional understanding of dyslexia, and how to educate 20 percent of the students in their charge.

MYTH 9: Dyslexia accommodations are unfair to other students.

TRUTH: Providing accommodations such as extra time or alternative methods of assessment of knowledge (an oral exam or project instead of a written exam, for example) levels the playing field for students with dyslexia in relation to their peers. It does not provide an unfair advantage.

MYTH 10: Dyslexia prevents students from attending college.

TRUTH: While many students with dyslexia are discouraged by the high-stakes testing necessary to gain entry and the potential challenges of higher education, students with dyslexia can succeed in college. It may be the first time in their schooling that they have a voice in choosing their classes and can pursue a course of study that interests them.

Dyslexia History 101

Dyslexia was first called "word blindness," an unfortunate term coined in 1877 by German neurologist Adolph Kussmaul, who observed that some of his patients had difficulty reading properly, and noted: "A complete text-blindness may exist, although the power of sight, the intellect, and the powers of speech are intact."

A decade later, Rudolf Berlin, an ophthalmologist in Stuttgart, introduced the term "dyslexia" to replace "word blindness." That term further added to the confusion about dyslexia, perpetuating the misconception that it is an issue of vision rather than processing in the brain.

In 1896, English physician, W. Pringle Morgan wrote about dyslexia in the British Medical Journal: "Percy ... aged 14 ... has always been a bright and intelligent boy, quick at games, and in no way inferior to others of his age. His great difficulty has been—and is now—his inability to read."

Anna Gillingham, a progressive educator at the Ethical Culture School in New York City during the 1930s, addressed the many challenges faced by bright children who struggled to read. "As such children grow older they are either eliminated from the school altogether or they gradually acquire sufficient reading ability to go along after a fashion," she wrote. "This usually means that they are no longer regarded as non-readers, at least not as more than slow readers: they are poor in textbook study; they cannot spell, they cannot express ideas readily and clearly in written symbols; they plunge into repeated failing in foreign language study. Through all this their emotional factors are intensified."

Gillingham teamed with neurologist Dr. Samuel Orton at Columbia University and the two pioneers developed a successful reading program to help students. Their enthusiasm for helping students with dyslexia is obvious when they reported: "No other appeal is to us stronger than that of the student whose keen mind and eager desire, perhaps real gift in literary style and imagination, are imprisoned by his awkwardness with the language tools. We feel that in no other way is our work more needed than in the liberation of those minds and souls from the bondage of their own specific disabilities."

The Orton-Gillingham approach, as it's now known, is an intensive, phonics-based, multi-sensory approach that involves three pathways of learning: visual, auditory, and kinesthetic. It is a successful approach for all learners, not just those with dyslexia, because it teaches to students' strengths while improving their weaknesses. It remains the standard work from which other effective programs for students with dyslexia are derived including Wilson, Slingerland, and Barton. Orton and Gillingham's first manual, *Remedial Training for Children with Specific Disability in Reading, Spelling and Penmanship,* was published in 1935; it continues to be updated and revised.

Their work formed the basis of The Orton Dyslexia Society, now the International Dyslexia Association. The mission of the nonprofit educational and advocacy organization is "to pursue and provide the most comprehensive range of information and services that address the full scope of dyslexia and related difficulties in learning to read and write. . . in a way that creates hope, possibility, and partnership."

Reading Wars

The Punic Wars (264 BC to 146 BC) fought between Rome and Carthage went on for 82 years.

The Phonics Wars (1920 AD to the present) have been going on for nearly 100 years with no end in sight.

Some of the most ferocious fighting in the Phonics Wars took place in 1955 when Austrian educator Rudolf Flesch wrote *Why Johnny Can't Read: and what you can do about it*. His bestseller (imagine that!) set out a compelling argument about the superiority of what he called the "phonics first" approach to reading and spelling, over the "whole word" approach, that encourages guessing, rather than understanding the phonetic principles of the English language.

Flesch emphasized the need to explicitly teach the basics of the English language through phonics, as well as the sounds of vowels, consonants, specific combinations, and irregular words. Phonics, Flesch pointed out, had a far better track record in teaching all students—including different learners such as those with dyslexia—than the Whole Language method.

While popular with parents, *Why Johnny Can't Read* was met with a fusillade of criticism from educators. Phonics partisans were bombarded by the heavy artillery of the Education Establishment and forced to withdraw their troops from the frontlines in the First and Second grades. Just as the Roman Empire eventually crushed the Phoenicians, the Education Establishment crushed the Phonicians. Whole Languagers took over schools and schools systems across the nation, and the teaching of phonics and the basics of the structure and sounds of the language was all but abandoned.

Phonics supporters retreated to scattered strongholds, where they continued practicing their traditional beliefs and successfully teaching their children to read.

Twenty-six years later, in 1981 the Phonics Wars flared up again when Flesch wrote a powerful follow-up volume to *Why Johnny Can't Read*, titled *Why Johnny Still Can't Read: A New Look at the Scandal of our Schools*. In it, he reiterated the need to teach "phonics first" instead of what he called "look and say," which forces students to get clues from photos or drawings that may accompany the text, or rely on memorization or simple guesswork when encountering unfamiliar words—with no way to relate the sounds to the letters, or decode the blends.

Whole Languagers put down this uprising, but 26 *more* years later, they faced another when the Phonics forces revolted again. In 1997, Congress appointed the National Reading Panel to conduct a comprehensive study to determine the effectiveness of various approaches to teaching children to read. The panel concluded: *teaching phonics was beneficial for all readers across the board.*

The Reading Wars continue to this day. Armed only with facts, science, and a proven methodology, Phonics supporters are still no match for the Educational Establishment, which stubbornly embraces the Whole Language approach. Phonics adherents continue to point out that reading is the ability to interpret a code— the letters on a page that represent sounds. When students with dyslexia are specifically taught how to break the code, they can read.

Opponents of phonics use such approaches as "context clues," "guided reading" and "balanced literacy," with emphasis on "sight words," which offer little or no explicit instruction in the structure, sounds, and meaning of the English language.

These approaches are *not* appropriate for students with dyslexia because they do not teach them how to decode. They are an updated continuation of the Whole Language approach that Flesch decried so long ago, but lives on.

According to the Nation's Report Card (2015), only 36 percent of 4th graders score proficient or above in reading; 34 percent of 8th graders score proficient or above and just 37 percent of 12th graders score proficient or above. So much for the effectiveness of the Whole Language Approach.

Twentieth-Century Dyslexia Pioneers

During the 1950s, at a time of great social and cultural conformity, a significant number of parents realized that their bright and curious children were wilting in the relentless uniformity of a public school system that was failing to teach them reading, writing, and arithmetic.

Few of these parents realized their children were dyslexic or knew anything abut dyslexia and were horrified when told by the Education Establishment that their children's brains were defective, that they needed to be placed in "special" classes with students with severe cognitive impairments, and likely would never graduate from high school. Many parents were told, in the acceptable vocabulary of the times, that their children were "mentally retarded."

These parents knew instinctively that the Educational Establishment was wrong, rejected its conclusions, and took matters into their own hands. Sometimes traveling long distances, they took their children to research centers at hospitals and universities where they were hooked up to wires and studied by scientists.

These parents educated themselves with the limited information available at the time, demanded their children have access to "regular" classes in school, and spent small fortunes outside of schools on private tutors, private schools, eye exercises, special lenses, re-learning to crawl, manipulating limbs, throwing bean bags, walking on beams, reading with a metronome, and anything else the "experts" recommended.

A lucky few discovered, in the second half of the 20th century, that the Orton-Gillingham approach to reading was what these kids needed, and they set about learning everything they could about it, and how to provide it for their children.

Dedicated parents and dyslexia advocates began sharing their hard-won dyslexia knowledge with others by establishing nonprofits, summer camps, schools, and training centers. At a time when knowledge of dyslexia was far less widespread than it is today, these individuals received training in outposts near and far—and shared it with the world.

Let us recognize these pioneers and unsung heroes—many with dyslexia themselves—who have made great impact by training others and working tirelessly with empathy and goodwill to help make their part of the world more dyslexia-friendly. Among them are:

Teaching those with dyslexia: Beth Slingerland who taught in Hawaii and moved to Washington, where she developed the Slingerland approach to reading; Roger

Saunders who helped establish the Odyssey School in Baltimore and the Rawson-Saunders School in Austin, Texas; and Dr. Luke Waites, who was so influential in connecting the Scottish Rite to dyslexia back in 1965, that their dyslexia clinic in Dallas was named for him.

School founders: Peter Gow of the Gow School in New York in 1926; Diana Hanbury King who co-founded the Kildonan School in Pennsylvania in 1950; Marianne Frostig, who founded the Frostig School in Los Angeles in 1951; David Schenck, who founded the Schenck School in Atlanta in the early 1960s. Others include Dr. Charles Armstrong, who founded the Menlo Clinic and inspired Dr. Wilbur Mattison to establish the Charles Armstrong School in Menlo Park, CA in 1968 (now located in Belmont); Joyce Bilgrove and David Malin who founded Camp Jemicy that became Jemicy School in Baltimore in the early 1970s, and Charles Drake who founded the Landmark School in Massachusetts in 1971. (All of these fine educational establishments are still serving students with dyslexia to this day.)

Learn more about dyslexia pioneers from the International Dyslexia Association's "Hall of Honor" (dyslexia.org).

National Politics

From local school boards to state legislatures to the U.S. Congress, education in America is politically driven. Positions and policies embraced by an individual politician toward dyslexia are influenced by factors that include ideology and powerful interest groups as well as personal and family experiences with dyslexia.

Institutional resistance to addressing dyslexia at the highest political levels is exemplified by an exchange between Sen. Bill Cassidy (R-LA) and then-Secretary of Education Arne Duncan during a Congressional hearing. (Note: Cassidy is the parent of a child with dyslexia who established a public dyslexia charter school and pushed for improvements in student testing and teacher training in dyslexia in his home state.) In a classic political dance performance, Duncan skipped and tiptoed around direct questions about dyslexia.

Cassidy: "What specific programs does the department fund for dyslexia?"

Duncan: "I don't think we have a specific program for dyslexia…"

Cassidy: "…Why the heck don't we have a special program for students with dyslexia?"

Duncan: "…Something for Congress to think about…there are many children with special needs…"

Cassidy chaired a Senate committee hearing about dyslexia to raise awareness on the scope, scale, and science of dyslexia, as well as the importance of early identification.

State Politics

The United States of DyslexiaLand is anything but united in its approach to dyslexia. Each state has its own way of interpreting the Individuals with Disabilities Education Act, and how it addresses dyslexia.

New Jersey, Mississippi, Ohio, Arkansas, Arizona, Washington, Indiana, and New York recently passed dyslexia legislation, and more states are following suit.

Passing meaningful dyslexia legislation is a challenge to say to the least, as a recent political fight in California illustrates. California Assembly Member Jim Frazier introduced legislation in 2015 to address dyslexia comprehensively—with provisions for early identification, teacher training, evidence-based reading programs and an improved definition of dyslexia in the state's Education Code. It was strongly supported by Decoding Dyslexia-CA, parents and education advocates throughout the state.

Through the political process, the bill was significantly amended, due to strong opposition by organizations representing teachers, school boards and special education administrators. These special interest groups succeeded in eliminating the important provisions for early identification and teacher training from the legislation.

The bill was signed into law by Gov. Jerry Brown in the fall of 2015. It allows students to qualify for Special

Education services in the category of "phonological processing," and developed new dyslexia guidelines, that provide a roadmap for educators to follow, adding to the dialogue about dyslexia at the district level throughout the state. The guidelines suggest that dyslexic students who don't qualify for Special Education should still be supported in general education classrooms.

Local Politics

School districts are required to implement state and federal education codes, but often interpret their missions quite differently. Districts develop reputations—positive and negative—for how they implement Special Education services and how they approach dyslexia. Much of this depends on the vision and leadership of its top administration, as well as the training of the teaching staff and the perspective and background knowledge of the superintendent.

Because they are elected members of the community, school boards are supposed to question and responsibly oversee the actions of the school district they serve. The relationship between the school board and the superintendent is a crucial one: one that is either too contentious or too cozy spells trouble for the community.

A recent example of Los Angeles Unified School District is instructive about how board members can lead administrators in a new direction. A couple of motivated mothers, who also happened to be teachers, approached school board members with their concerns about dyslexia in the schools. The school board members passed a resolution designating October as Dyslexia Awareness Month and directed the superintendent to develop a comprehensive approach to dyslexia and to report back to the board within 60 calendar days. Their exemplary action resulted in the establishment of four task forces, comprised of parents and educators, working collaboratively to address dyslexia.

School districts, and those who staff and run them, wield a great deal of power in their local communities: they make crucial decisions about educational priorities; program funding; educators' experience and training; graduation requirements; reading approaches; and dozens of other important aspects of public education. They also have great economic and social impact on a community, with the ability to float bond measures, control the public relations narrative, and receive support from community leaders and the philanthropic class.

When those who run the local school district are ill-informed about dyslexia, they may make funding and policy decisions that are short-sighted in understanding the ultimate individual and societal costs of their failure to address it. At some point, parents may decide to speak up and speak out in order to make a positive difference for the 1 in 5 with dyslexia.

STRESSFUL

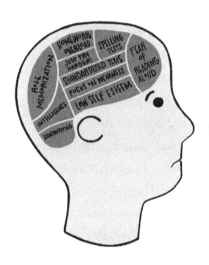

SUCCESSFUL

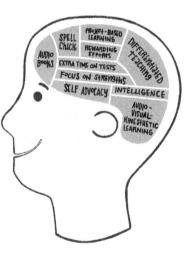

4

Mind Maps of Dyslexia
From Stressful to Successful

The demands of a school setting and curriculum are stressful for students with dyslexia. Parents and teachers may have high academic performance expectations for them, particularly when they are obviously bright and capable. When their intelligence is not reflected in their test scores, writing assignments or ability to read, these expectations often turn to blame with accusations that the student with dyslexia is just not trying hard enough.

Imagine hearing that?! Especially if you have put heart and soul into the work, believing that the results will be positive. It is deeply soul-crushing and self-defeating—especially when students with dyslexia are among the hardest-working students of all.

Students with dyslexia are stressed in ways that might not even occur to their classmates, parents or teachers, as the mind map illustrates.

Stressful with Dyslexia

Fear of Reading Aloud: Dyslexia, aka "the invisible disability," becomes a visible one, and painfully obvious when a student with dyslexia is required to read aloud in class. Dyslexic students may go to great lengths to avoid reading aloud, and come up with all kinds of excuses: "needing" to go to the bathroom or saying they forgot their (non-existent) glasses or contact lenses. The most common response is attempting to quickly memorize the passage they think they will have to read. This memorizing strategy falls apart if the preceding student reads a little more or a little less text, and may throw our reader with dyslexia into a panic.

Spelling: Figuring out the proper combination of letters to represent sounds and words is the bane of existence for students with dyslexia. In the typical classroom, the ability to spell is considered an important indicator of intelligence. It's not.

Many students with dyslexia (and many without!) will never figure out the confounding difference between way and weigh, ate and eight, or son and sun—yet they will be evaluated on their ability to remember homonyms and spell words that "break the rules."

Homework Overload: After a long day of school, students with dyslexia are often forced to struggle through an equally long night of homework; answering questions on worksheets; trying to solve too many equations; and dealing with lists of spelling and vocabulary words, then trying to get it all finished for the next day—when it starts all over again. Studies suggest "busywork" assignments add little to schooling, or ultimately, to knowledge, and they certainly have a negative effect on a struggling student's enthusiasm for learning.

Just Try Harder: Every student with dyslexia hears this phrase countless times. And no one seems to listen when they reply, "I am trying as hard as I can." The "Blame the Student" syndrome is rampant, particularly in secondary school, among teachers who just don't get it that the student is already doing the best job possible, and may have made it to high school while reading at a primary school level. For the student with dyslexia, the inability to perform well on a reading-and-writing-based assignment is likely an indication of difficulties producing work that reflects acquired knowledge, not willful disobedience.

Rote Memorization: Drilling facts and figures into the head of a student with dyslexia just doesn't work. Learning the multiplication tables is typically difficult for these students. Multi-sensory teaching methods work better, such as the use of rhyme schemes, visualizing techniques, hands-on projects and kinesthetic exercises.

Standardized Tests: These tests may assess the knowledge and performance skills of a typical student. But even the brightest student with dyslexia may reveal a significant discrepancy between intelligence (and knowledge), and the ability to show it on standardized tests, where deciphering the question, reading the paragraphs and filling in the proper responses—under time pressures—are required.

Handwriting: Difficulty writing (dysgraphia) often accompanies dyslexia. Forming letters, spacing words, and lining up sentences and paragraphs can be an arduous experience—with results that are often illegible.

Focus on Weaknesses: Today's classroom emphasis on reading, writing, spelling and math—with note-taking from lectures, filling out worksheets, writing drills, organizational requirements and constant written assessments does not accurately measure the knowledge gained, or indicate the abilities of a student with dyslexia.

Low Self-Esteem: The daily grind in school where a student with dyslexia experiences multiple failures is virtually guaranteed to negatively affect self confidence, increase anxiety, and lower self-esteem. Difficulties getting needed accommodations, and then having them implemented further beat down students with dyslexia. Special Education has a way of making students feel "special" for all the wrong reasons, and may even cause students to avoid using their accommodations so they don't attract attention for being different.

Unappreciated Intelligence: Underlying it all is the intelligence of the student with dyslexia that is overlooked, un-realized and under-appreciated. The same student may excel in all manner of other abilities, interests and activities that are just not the focus of the assessments or education going on in the classroom.

Successful with Dyslexia

When students with dyslexia are taught in the way they learn, they have a reasonable opportunity for success in school. Providing them with appropriate accommodations, reading programs and assistive technologies changes everything for students with dyslexia.

Audiobooks: Instead of struggling to read their school assignments, students with dyslexia can make use of wonderful improvements in access to technology—as well as enlightened thinking on the subject that makes no judgment about how they access the material. What difference does it make if a student accesses print by reading with their eyes, with their fingers (Braille) or with their ears? Students with dyslexia can cover much more reading material when they have access to audio versions of textbooks, novels and other class assignments. Online access to these audio versions includes Bookshare, audible.com and Learning Ally, among others.

Spell Check: Eliminate the issues of misspellings and illegible handwriting by allowing the student to use technological solutions, including spell check, speech-to-text and text-to-speech programs. Google, Siri, and Alexa can be a great help!

Project-Based Learning: Students with dyslexia are often skilled at understanding classroom lessons, and hands-on approaches allow them to engage with the material. They may also excel in demonstrating their knowledge by creating projects. Verbal exams, making videos, designing web pages, composing songs and creating artwork are ways of expressing knowledge other than by the conventional manner of writing essays or taking multiple choice tests.

Rewarding Effort: As a counter to "Just try harder," and the insistence on completion of every single problem on nightly worksheets and homework, the recognition of hard work completed and shortened homework assignments can be very beneficial for students with dyslexia.

Extra Time on Tests: This most common accommodation makes a huge difference for the student with dyslexia who just needs additional time to process the questions, and to complete the work on a typical exam.

Differentiated Teaching: Today's typical classroom is filled with students who have different ways of learning yet are all being taught in the exact same way. The most successful teachers have learned to present lessons in multiple ways so that the material is accessible to everyone in the class, no matter what their learning style.

Audio-Visual Kinesthetic Learning: Make the best use of a student's learning style. For creative problem-solvers, consider simulations of real-world problems that must be solved by big-thinking, cooperation and skillful negotiations. For kinesthetic learners, consider hands-on classes in woodworking, art, jewelry-making and the like. Visual learners can create expressive projects that interpret literature or history lessons.

Focus on Strengths: The student with dyslexia (all-too-often seen as a collection of failures in school) should be encouraged to pursue talents, interests and skills outside the classroom—and use them inside the classroom as well. This is a confidence builder; it provides a platform for success and a way to engage in the project. In my son's case, for example, he utilized his love of baseball throughout his years of school, and used baseball-oriented projects whenever possible—from science experiments (wood bat vs. metal bat) to book reports (biographies of ballplayers).

Self-Advocacy: Owning dyslexia is the best way of all for a student to get through DyslexiaLand. Understanding this unique learning style—and being able to communicate it to others—allows for a sense of empowerment about how to work with others.

Intelligence: It's time adults get smart about dyslexia. Students with dyslexia can reveal their true intelligence in the classroom when their learning style is understood, and they are taught in the way they learn.

5

Mapping a Pathway
Through DyslexiaLand
Obstacles and Opportunities

Obstacles

DyslexiaLand can be a dull, mysterious and confusing world for students who learn differently—and for those charged with educating them. This land is too-often characterized by a swirl of indecipherable jargon that leads to misunderstandings, denial and even behavioral issues.

The confusingly non-specific diagnosis of "Specific Learning Disability" for their child is baffling to parents determined, even desperate, to understand what to do and how to help.

Processing issues: Students with dyslexia are often identified with issues in "visual processing," "auditory processing" or "memory processing." These terms, rarely defined and confusing—particularly in the stressful setting of an IEP meeting—obscure the recognition of dyslexia and slow the development of implementing appropriate plans for the student with dyslexia.

Spelling bees: The standard game in many classrooms is no fun at all for students with dyslexia for whom spelling is a swarm of letters. These kids can still participate by keeping score or opting out in order to avoid the sting of embarrassment and repeated failure.

Timed tests: Timed tests add another level of difficulty for students with dyslexia. Providing extra time—typically 1.5 to two times more—is the most common accommodation to help level the assessment playing field. Other options include verbal, rather than written tests, use of student-created notes, or an alternate setting for exam.

Pop quiz: The suddenness and lack of ability to prepare—usually requiring quick recall of facts and figures—are added impediments for students with dyslexia.

Ton of homework: After a full day of school, the last thing a student with dyslexia needs or wants is more schoolwork. Reducing the amount of work (assigning every other problem, for example), reducing the number of questions or problem on a page so they're not overwhelming; and offering additional time to complete the work are all successful strategies to lighten the homework load. Often teachers prove more flexible than you might imagine; an option to nightly homework could be that students request that the student meet once a week or every two weeks with the teacher and verbally prove understanding of the material covered—without completing every bit of homework assigned on paper.

Behavioral issues: Students with dyslexia may end up with behavioral issues because they're covering up their learning differences, or because they just can't handle the stresses in the classroom. This can lead to real trouble, especially in the teen years, when all sorts of feel-good temptations are so easy to obtain—and when skipping class seems like a reasonable alternative to a miserable classroom situation.

Emotional Toll Booth/Humiliation Hills: Repeatedly failing to measure up to expectations, as is the case for many students with dyslexia, takes a serious emotional toll. Their loss of self-esteem and "feeling dumb" may define and affect every aspect of their lives in school—and extend into adulthood, becoming a self-fulfilling prophecy.

Specific Learning Disability/Jargon: The umbrella term of Specific Learning Disability, and the rampant use of acronyms (SLD, IEP, ISEA, SPED, etc.) in the special education community is confusing for parents. When these terms fly around and are neither defined nor understood, it's very difficult to move forward and get appropriate assistance.

Mountain of Paperwork/Bureaucratic Swamp: All too often, official attempts to assist students through special education services end up mired in the stilted legal and bureaucratic requirements of documentation and written requests, along with specifications of timing and the use of language—all of which can be daunting to even the most determined parent.

Standardization/Rote Route: Memorization, recall of small details, and the typical standardized tests will not necessarily assess the knowledge a student with dyslexia has gained in the course of study.

Boxed in/Muddy Waters/Alphabet Soup: Students with dyslexia often flounder in classrooms that focus on their weaknesses and ignore their strengths. This severely compromises their ability to achieve in the academic environment, leading far too often to students' loss of interest, shutting down, or even dropping out of school—a place where they may feel they don't belong.

River of Denial: Too often parents hear that everything will be fine, that classroom issues will work themselves out if they just give them enough time. For the student with dyslexia, without proven interventions, support and instruction, problems in school will likely only get worse. There's no denying it.

Land of Lost Potential: Dyslexia is no reason to keep students from reaching their full potential. If they receive the specific approaches to reading, writing and math that will support their learning style, they have every opportunity to succeed. If not, their academic promise may be overlooked, cutting them off from pathways to success.

Opportunities

Bridge to Understanding: There is a way out of the dark and confusing place for the student with dyslexia. It comes from understanding this learning difference, providing appropriate accommodations, instruction and access to technology, and realizing how parents and educators can team to help students with dyslexia.

Informed Parents + Knowledgeable Educators = Empowered Students: DyslexiaLand becomes a bright and lively place when information and awareness about dyslexia is embraced by parents and educators as they guide these 1 in 5 students on their journey to reach their full potential. It's a collaborative process that requires teamwork, communication, flexibility and learning on everyone's part—maybe even getting parents and educators to think far out of their comfort zone and deeply held beliefs.

Evidence-Based Strategies: Although it may seem so, it's not rocket science to properly educate students with dyslexia. Research on the subject dates back to the 1930s, and continues to evolve with a structured approach to reading, writing, and spelling. Appropriate teaching strategies, programs, systems, and information is widely available and disseminated in scholarly journals, online, and even in popular culture—everywhere, it seems, sometimes, except in the typical classroom.

Courage/Determination/Persistence: These personal qualities, so often characteristic of students with dyslexia, help in creating their success—far beyond the classroom walls. Adults need to recognize and encourage the effort and work put forth by these different thinkers who work so hard with so little reward.

Out of the Box/Collaboration Corner/3-D Thinking/Big Ideas: Students with dyslexia perceive the world very differently than others. They excel in situations where they can unleash their imaginations, work with others and come up with innovative solutions to daunting problems. People with dyslexia thrive in a place where vision and opportunity meet, and where creative problem-solving is encouraged and rewarded.

Assistive Technology/iPad/SpellCheck: Access to innovations in our digital world have improved the lives of students with dyslexia immeasurably: today's technology provides tools unimaginable just a dozen years ago, with the power of the iPad and other tablets, smartphones and apps specifically designed to improve the lives of those who have dyslexia. Allowing students access to Assistive Technology (AT) simplifies their lives and should be encouraged: Speech-to-text, text-to-speech, audio books, note-taking, writing assistance, text-editing and more. Research the latest tech, and determine what works best for your child! Make sure your child receives appropriate instruction when introduced to AT.

Role Models: These days so many individuals who struggled in school are willing to share their stories! Many rich and famous people with dyslexia are outspoken about how they succeeded in life after early difficulties. Equally important are community role models with dyslexia who are neither rich nor famous, but who have found a measure of happiness and success and who are willing to speak up. When they share their stories, young people identify with them, and they help create more understanding about dyslexia in every phase of life.

Proper Accommodations/Alternative Assessments/Notes Provided: In the ideal setting, students with dyslexia are offered the accommodations necessary to "level the playing field" that allows them to access educational materials and resources like every other student. Proven accommodations may include extra time on tests; alternative settings for exams, projects and homework; reduced homework assignments; verbal exams instead of multiple choice or essays; preferential seating; no peer-grading and no reading out loud unless the student volunteers. Accommodations are particularly effective when implemented proactively, matter-of-factly, and with the full support of the classroom teacher without bringing undue attention to the student. Parents must work creatively and collaboratively with the 504 or IEP team to develop appropriate accommodations.

Multi-Sensory Learning/Audio-Visual/Music/Art/ Sports: Students with dyslexia flourish when taught in ways that enhance their strengths and do not focus on their challenges with the written word. Classroom activities such as simulations that require collaboration and innovative thinking, as well as developing strategies for solving real-world problems are very good for these students. Participation in classes and campus activities in which they can excel such as music, the arts, robotics and engineering, student government, sports, outdoor recreation, woodshop and other hands-on activities helps students with dyslexia enjoy success and cope with the challenges of the classroom.

Entrepreneurial Spirit / Creative Cove / Smooth Sailing / Hope Springs: Individuals with dyslexia often possess the innovative vision and the creative prob-lem-solving skills that make for successful entrepreneurs. Provide encouragement and classroom support for what is obviously a great strength in the business world. It's estimated that more than one-third of the highly success-ful entrepreneurs have dyslexia.

Land of Full Potential: Dyslexia should be seen as a difference, not a disability, to allow maximum growth, educational accomplishment, and personal fulfillment that lasts a lifetime.

PART II

PARENT EMPOWERMENT ZONE

Children with dyslexia who attend most public schools are square pegs forced into round holes. A one-size-fits-all, standardized approach doesn't work for them. It wastes potential and ruins lives in the futile process of forcing them to conform to a public education system that hasn't been built for the way they think, learn, and express themselves.

Longtime dyslexia advocates agree: School officials are not likely to tell parents what they need to know in order to help their dyslexic children. Therefore parents *must* adopt a strategy to get optimal assistance, and learn to advocate to acquire these services.

When parents become educated about dyslexia, they are more likely to speak up, and to seek out and acquire the specialized help their children need. Unfortunately, far too often that parental education takes place after months, or more likely, years of false hopes and empty reassurances that everything will be fine—when clearly it is not.

No easy options are available for parents in search of a quality education for their child with dyslexia. A lucky few have access to public schools with enlightened leadership that have programs in place to teach students with dyslexia in the way they learn. An increasing number are turning to a variety of home-school methods and programs. Parents able to afford the high tuition can send their children to private schools designed for students with dyslexia. More affordable, but still costly, options for parents are intensive programs and both short-term and long-term specialized tutoring.

Unless parents opt for private school or home-schooling, they need to commit to hands-on management of their child's public school education. In order to do so, parents must learn to become effective advocates. For those who may have learning differences or language barriers of their own, advocacy may not come easily.

Best advice for parents who advocate for their child is the same advice offered students:

* **Go to school:** Learn what you don't know.

* **Stay in school:** Learn what you need to know.

* **Do your homework**: Research, do the busywork, turn your papers in on time,

* **Work together:** Figure out who you need to know, and how to work with them; develop a network of support.

* **Timing is everything:** Know the school calendar, learn who you need to meet when for what reason.

* **Know the law:** Research and understand the legal requirements that schools must follow to address the needs of dyslexic students.

6

Recognizing Dyslexia

"**M**y son *can't* have dyslexia. He doesn't see things backwards. He just has trouble taking tests, writing and spelling."

"The teacher said that dyslexia is a medical issue, not an educational one. If I want to find out if my child has dyslexia, I have to go to the pediatrician and get a referral so I can get a diagnosis from a neuropsychologist, and my insurance doesn't cover it. It will cost around $3,500 for that testing, and I don't have that kind of money."

"I don't know what it is about my daughter, but she is so thoughtful and compassionate with her friends, and she's so creative with her interest in drama, dance, singing and playing the piano. There's just something special about her. But she just cannot handle school."

Recognizing dyslexia is often presented as a difficult and confusing task, one that baffles parents—as well as the educational community, and even the medical establishment. It need not be so confusing, because parents who observe their children—and trust their intuition—can pick up on the signs of dyslexia long before they're detected in school through a battery of tests. Many of these signs indicate great strengths in a child's development, not just academic struggles.

Positive attributes of dyslexia tend to manifest early in a child's development: Big-picture and 3-D thinking, creative and spatial abilities, a highly developed sense of intuition and empathy, and a real aptitude with project-based, hands-on learning.

Sometimes it takes far too long to recognize dyslexia, even in the case of very accomplished individuals. For example, financial wizard Charles Schwab didn't learn about his dyslexia until he was in his 40s; filmmaker Steven Spielberg didn't learn about his until he was 60! Both innovative thinkers recognized their own dyslexia when seeking help for their children who were struggling in school. Both spent far too many years thinking they just weren't very smart, due to their late identification.

Parents may think it's cute when their small children insist on mispronouncing words like "pisketti" for "spaghetti," "samwitch" for "sandwich" or "aminiamal" for "animal." And they may just roll their eyes at children who seem to take forever to learn to tie their shoes, remember how to spell their name, tell time on an analog clock, turn in their homework or keep their rooms tidy.

But all of these *may* be early indicators of dyslexia. Other signs include a family history; difficulty rhyming or sounding out words when reading aloud, or a mismatch between telling a story with rich detail and writing it down in stilted and abbreviated form.

The earlier dyslexia is recognized, the more opportunity there is to develop a pathway to success. Your child is not alone and neither is your family. Look around at your child's friends and classmates and remember: In every classroom, in every school, in every school district, 1 in 5 students has dyslexia.

What Dyslexia Is and Is Not

Dyslexia Is:

Dyslexia **is** a language-based learning difference rooted in the neurological wiring of the brain. It can be managed through understanding, appropriate instruction and experience, but not "cured."

Dyslexia **is** hereditary.

Dyslexia **is** characterized by difficulty decoding, manipulating and understanding written language and the sounds letters make.

Dyslexia **is** characteristic of innovators, engineers, inventors, athletes, artists, storytellers, entrepreneurs and many other individuals with extraordinary abilities to see and experience the world differently.

Dyslexia **is** a learning difference that often manifests as a disability in schools where it is not properly addressed and accommodated.

Dyslexia Is Not:

Dyslexia **is not** rare: It affects 1 in 5 individuals.

Dyslexia **is not** seeing letters or words backwards.

Dyslexia **is not** an indicator of lack of intelligence.

Dyslexia **is not** Attention Deficit Disorder, although ADD is often confused with dyslexia, particularly in school.

Dyslexia **is not** a disease. There is no "cure" or "solution." There are many great workarounds and ways to minimize its effects in daily life, but it does not "go away," as some think.

Dyslexia **is not** a disability. It is a learning difference. (However, in Special Ed, dyslexia is considered a disability and must be acknowledged as such in order to get services.)

Types of Dyslexia

Academics have named the types of dyslexia. These terms are not in common use. However, they're worth noting because dyslexia varies widely from person to person.

Dysphonetic dyslexia, also called auditory or phonological—which relates to the processing of the sounds of language. This is the difficulty in decoding language so very common in individuals with dyslexia.

Dyseidetic dyslexia, also called surface or visual— relates to the recognition of whole words and how to spell. It frequently causes difficulties in remembering sight words.

Stealth dyslexia, so named because it occurs in gifted individuals who have well-developed verbal skills, and may have their processing issues overlooked and unidentified for years.

Identifying Dyslexia

Indicators of dyslexia are nearly always presented as scary negatives—like those long lists of side effects at the end of TV commercials for drugs marketed by big pharmaceutical companies. Many positive indicators of dyslexia are also observable, and should be listed right alongside the negative ones; they are overlooked because they point to strengths not measured or particularly valued in school.

The indicators presented below are time-tested observations and a good start for parents to recognize dyslexia, but are not a substitute for a professional and comprehensive assessment.

Always keep the big picture in mind: individuals with dyslexia can have very happy, productive and successful lives, once dyslexia is recognized, and addressed effectively.

Pre-school Years

- ✓ delayed speech
- ✓ difficulty understanding sounds in words
- ✓ mixing up the sounds and syllables in long words
- ✓ chronic ear infections

- ✓ confusion of left versus right; late establishing a dominant hand
- ✓ difficulty learning to tie shoes
- ✓ trouble memorizing their address, phone number, or the alphabet
- ✓ difficulty rhyming
- ✓ a close relative with dyslexia

Elementary School Years

- ✓ dysgraphia (slow, non-automatic handwriting that is difficult to read)
- ✓ letter or number reversals continuing past the end of first grade
- ✓ difficulty learning cursive
- ✓ reading is slow, choppy, inaccurate:—guesses based on shape or context—skips or misreads prepositions (at, to, of)—ignores suffixes—can't sound out unknown words
- ✓ difficulty spelling
- ✓ often can't remember sight words (they, were, does) or homonyms (their, they're, and there)
- ✓ difficulty telling time with a clock with hands
- ✓ trouble with math—memorizing multiplication tables
- ✓ memorizing a sequence of steps—directionality
- ✓ when speaking, difficulty finding the correct word— lots of "whatyamacallits" and "thingies"—common sayings come out slightly twisted
- ✓ nightmares about school
- ✓ extremely messy bedroom, backpack, and desk

✓ dreads going to school
✓ complains of stomach aches or headaches

High School Years

Above characteristics plus:

✓ limited vocabulary
✓ extremely poor written expression
✓ large discrepancy between verbal skills and written compositions
✓ difficulty mastering a foreign language
✓ difficulty reading printed music
✓ poor grades in many classes
✓ may drop out of high school
✓ anxiety about school, future
✓ may ditch class, increase in behavior issues
✓ potential for substance abuse, juvenile justice issues, self-harming activities

Adult Years

Educational history similar to above, plus:

✓ slow reader
✓ may have to read a page several times to understand it
✓ difficulty putting thoughts onto paper—dreads writing memos or letters
✓ still has difficulty with right versus left
✓ may be underemployed
✓ may enlist others for proofreading, other assistance on the job

Look for These Strengths

- ✓ Outside the box thinking
- ✓ Understanding in 3-D
- ✓ Exceptional empathy and compassion
- ✓ Creativity
- ✓ Innovation
- ✓ Entrepreneurial skills
- ✓ Great storytelling
- ✓ Particular strengths and ability in the arts, science, building, athletics, big-picture concepts
- ✓ Desire to do well
- ✓ Persistence and determination
- ✓ Cleverness in creating workarounds to problem-solving

Who Determines Dyslexia?

When parents are informed about the characteristics of dyslexia, they do a good job of recognizing it in their children. But there's a difference between recognizing and identifying dyslexia and receiving a diagnosis for it. Educators may tell parents that dyslexia is a medical issue, rather than an educational one, and send parents to their pediatrician. This creates a ping-pong effect between the school and the doctor's office, since the pediatrician likely does not have the background or ability to address dyslexia, and will send the parent back to the school.

For an actual diagnosis of dyslexia, you may have to pay for a full work-up by an educational neuropsychologist experienced in dyslexia. This comprehensive evaluation provides excellent insight into a child's potential, abilities and difficulties. However a dyslexia work-up may come with two downsides: it can be quite costly and school officials may or may not accept it when it comes to providing services for dyslexia.

Since dyslexia is rarely addressed appropriately in the general education classroom, you may need to investigate Special Education. For your child to receive Special Education services for dyslexia at school, your child will need to be assessed. Testing performed by a school psychologist only determines qualification for services, not a diagnosis of dyslexia. However, a school psychologist can note that certain characteristics are consistent with dyslexia.

According to Federal law, parents are entitled to ask for an Independent Educational Evaluation (IEE) at public expense if they disagree with the results of the school testing. The district must comply or call a due process hearing in a timely manner. And the IEP team must consider the results of an outside assessment.

However, it is often the case that the school district will agree to pay only if the outside consultant comes from a list that they provide. Of course, since an IEE is like a second opinion, only more in-depth, it is important that it be conducted by a completely independent entity.

Talking With Children About Their Dyslexia

Some parents fear the "label" of dyslexia by educators, and worry that it will give permission to treat their child differently in school. Others worry about speaking with their children about dyslexia, for fear that they will be negatively affected. However, upon hearing they have dyslexia, most children express relief in the knowledge that there's a reason for their difficulties in the class-room. Having a name to put to it, learning that there are others, including many famous and accomplished individuals who also share dyslexia can be a source of empowerment and the beginning of self-advocacy.

I recommend that when parents initially speak with their child about dyslexia, they treat it as a special occasion, with an almost celebratory approach. Some parents take the child out for a special meal, have a tea party, or broach the conversation during a hike, or a walk in the park. Here's an example of how it could go:

"Sweetie, you know how you've been having trouble with your reading, and we had you tested? We'll what we found out is that you have something very interesting going on in your brain. It's wired a little bit differently, just like Uncle Bob, the airplane pilot and Grandma Mary, who is such a great artist.

"This difference is called 'dyslexia' and it's the reason you are so good at playing the guitar, while you still have so much trouble reading. A lot of people have dyslexia, and now that we know that you do, too, we will get you the right reading program to help you.

"So we're pretty excited to finally have an answer about all of this, and to get you the right approach to reading, writing and spelling. It may take a bit more time, and you'll have to work hard—like you always do—but having dyslexia means you're smart, you just think and learn a little differently. Oh, and let me tell you about lots of very famous who people have dyslexia…"

"Mom, does that mean I'm not dumb?"

"Oh, honey, you are absolutely not dumb. You are the smartest kid, and the hardest worker I know. We are going to make sure that everything works out just fine, now that we know about dyslexia!"

"Dyslexia. That sure is a silly word, but I'm glad to know there's a reason and that I'm not the only one. I feel better now."

"Thanks, honey. I do too."

7

Reading, Writing and Arithmetic

In the quiet classroom, a child stands up to take a turn at reading aloud. Slowly, the child guesses at the letters, blends and syllables. Classmates titter their amusement at what passes for reading, this unsuccessful attempt to decode word after word in a phrase, a sentence, a paragraph.

The child tries desperately to do as the teacher instructs: "Sound it out."

This well-meaning suggestion does no good. This child has no idea what sounds the letters make, alone or in combination.

The ordeal finally concludes at the end of the last line. The child collapses back into the hard chair, cloaked in humiliation, exposed to the core after voicing words that clunked and clattered against the ear. The cause is a neurological difference in the brain that we call dyslexia, the silent stalker that makes its presence known only when a bright child unexpectedly struggles to give voice to the printed word.

But this child doesn't know. This child's parents don't know. Worse, this child's teacher doesn't know either. All have begun to believe that the child is lazy, slow, unmotivated, resistant to figuring out how to make sense of the symbols on the page.

For a student with dyslexia, "sounding it out" does not come naturally. A dyslexic child lacks phonemic awareness, the understanding of the correlation between the alphabetical symbol and the sound it makes.

Children may keep the struggle quiet and hidden during individual reading time. But there's nowhere to go, no place to hide when it's time to read out loud.

Not that they don't try: They figure out creative ways to keep silent and shrink away from participating in class. They complain of a stomachache, the need for a drink of water or a trip to the bathroom the moment it's time to read out loud in class.

Anything, anything from revealing the shameful secret: *If you cannot read, you must be dumb.*

Reading Out Loud

Difficulty in reading aloud is often painfully recalled by adults with dyslexia as a source of great embarrassment, humiliation and even bullying, since most people assume that difficulty reading equates to low intelligence.

Parents and teachers must learn that it is not appropriate to allow a struggling child to be subjected to the inevitably upsetting and even traumatic experiences. Work instead with the child to develop reading skills so that one day he or she will be able to volunteer with confidence instead of dreading being called on.

Those classroom exercises known as "Round Robin" or "Popcorn Reading" are particularly anxiety producing for dyslexic children who are self-conscious about their struggles.

When they can't escape, they reveal all. While others glide over a page, struggling readers guess, stumble and haltingly plow, word-by-word through a single paragraph. It's painful for the listener, and even worse for the kids trying their best to get through the humiliating experience of reading aloud.

If they are lucky, no one whispers, laughs or points out their difficulties. But they know anyway, and long into adulthood they remember every agonizing moment when they are called upon to read a passage. I have met individuals with dyslexia in their 70s and 80s who have shared a reading nightmare dating back to a third-grade reading group.

As a sixth grader with dyslexia explained his experience: "When we're reading out loud in class, I sometimes look at a word and I say what I think it is, then read three more words, and realize it's wrong. So I go back and say it correctly and then I lose my thought. I don't really stay on the lines that much. I might get to the end of a sentence, and skip a line and then go back, and I'm all jumbled up and have to stop, and then I feel embarrassed."

Reading Challenges Revealed

The sounds of dyslexia are a giveaway: difficulties with simple articles like "a," "an" and "the," as well as the inability to read the same word when it appears two or three times in a paragraph. Dyslexic readers engage in outright guessing, come up with words completely out of context, and don't recognize rhyme schemes. They read with a painful, choppy, halting cadence utterly devoid of rhythm or fluidity.

Listen up, and speak out on behalf of this child. Because what will happen if no one offers the right kind of help is this: The child will sit down, shut up, and do everything possible to remain unnoticed—or may act out frustrations and develop behavior problems.

Reading issues may come as a surprise to parents when by all outward appearances their child appears bright, confident and talented in other areas—music, dance, sports, building projects and more—but is tentative and performs poorly on the academic work in the classroom.

Similarly, classroom teachers—who know a child is smart—may have difficulty comprehending why a child with obvious talent and intelligence cannot grasp the concepts of reading, spelling, or good penmanship. Too often that difficulty is interpreted as a motivation issue, or even a symptom of attention deficit issues. Boredom or failure to engage due to poor skills is often misinterpreted as ADD or ADHD. Teachers may even suggest that parents take their child to a pediatrician for medication in order to be successful in the classroom.

Most parents and many educators assume that reading mastery is a natural process achieved with relative ease at predictable developmental stages. Toddlers have been known to crack the code on their own, which only reinforces the belief that reading is a natural human activity. It is not. Advances in neuroscience confirm the human brain is hard-wired for verbal communication, not for reading the written word.

Often there is a huge discrepancy from how a child reads and how a child speaks. When assessed in the seventh grade, my son was reading at a second grade level, yet had the working vocabulary of a typical 18-year old. It baffled nearly everyone: a boy who struggled mightily to read was able converse easily and at a high level with adults.

Educators not schooled in the recognition of dyslexia, or who are unfamiliar with teaching strategies necessary to teach students with dyslexia, may just encourage the child to slow down and to try harder to sound out the words. Parents will be told to read more at home. (Reading at home is a great activity for many reasons, but it is no substitute for proper instruction to address the development of reading skills in a dyslexic student.)

Students with dyslexia can learn to read, but require a multisensory structured language approach such as Orton-Gillingham that incorporates a good deal of one-on-one instruction and significant repetition. Too often, students with dyslexia are not identified, or are expected to learn to read using ineffective programs that just waste their time. Repeated failures undermine their confidence and impede further progress.

Students with dyslexia can learn to read proficiently, if taught *differently* and *appropriately.* It's not a mystery and it's not confusing; it's about as straightforward as it gets: Give these kids an Orton-Gillingham approach to reading, add in some Structured Word Inquiry—to help them understand the roots, prefixes and suffixes of words—and watch them learn to read, write and spell.

Don't and they won't.

Reading is a Complicated Skill

Proficiency in reading requires the development of multiple skills that include word attack, decoding, fluency, comprehension, understanding of language structure, building vocabulary, sight recognition and phonemic awareness—and more! Students with dyslexia need explicit instruction in order to master these skills that do not come naturally to them. Dyslexic students are not "slow" readers; they are different readers.

Yet the reading programs typically offered to them in public school are designed for students who are slow to pick up reading skills, or who are English Language Learners who have different needs altogether. These distinctions in approaches to reading are important for parents to know, yet they are rarely discussed in schools or with classroom teachers—where far too many have no educational background in specific approaches to teaching reading to struggling dyslexic readers.

Too often, struggling readers in a classroom are given "extra help" in the back of the room by well-meaning community volunteers or para-educators who have a minimal amount of training in teaching reading. These students seem hopeless in such a setting, but would soar under the tutelage of a well-trained and highly experienced reading specialist with the ability to discern the child's needs.

Why Most Public Schools Can't Teach Children with Dyslexia to Read

✳ Most teachers receive little or no college training in dyslexia and arrive in the classroom inadequately prepared to recognize the signs of dyslexia or to instruct students with dyslexia. School districts rarely provide the unprepared teachers they employ with the kind of training needed to help kids with dyslexia. This lack of proper teacher training can lead to…well, let's be kind and call it a certain defensiveness on the part of teachers and school officials who do not want to reveal their lack of knowledge about dyslexia or their inability to provide appropriate instruction.

✳ Most school districts purchase reading programs based on what educators call a "balanced literary approach" rather than investing in an "evidence-based, structured, multi-sensory approach" (such as Orton-Gillingham) needed by students with dyslexia. When dyslexic students do not grasp how to read, write, and spell with these programs, they quickly fall behind their peers, and hit a wall at about the third-grade level.

✳ Rather than investing in proper training and implementing approaches that work to teach kids with dyslexia in the way that they learn, teachers and school officials insist on piecemeal approaches and programs known to be ineffective. When these methods don't work, students are redirected to Special Education; unless a proven program, provided by a trained teacher is implemented with fidelity, students with dyslexia won't get appropriate instruction there, either.

Reading Programs
That Don't Work and Why

Academic publishing is Big Business. Nicely boxed sets of reading materials, sometimes called "teachers' toolkits" are sold to educators by publishers' reps, who market their product with slickly produced brochures and videos, color-coded readers, and the promises of rigor, positive learning trajectories and literacy for all. In order to make the sale, they must get approval from school district decision-makers who expect a return on their investment.

Many of those decision-makers (which may include administrators, textbook/curriculum materials purchasers, school board members and classroom teachers) are insufficiently informed about the science of reading, or how to discern the crucial differences among the reading programs marketed to them. They may hear—and believe—sales pitches about how this or that new and improved reading program is research-based and meets the needs of all students in their district, including so-called "slow learners," struggling readers, English Language Learners, and students in Special Education. What district decision-makers usually fail to consider is that the program they're buying, supposedly designed to teach all students, will do nothing at all for the 1 in 5 students with dyslexia.

School districts invest hundreds of thousands—even millions—of dollars in reading programs, spending the entire reading budget to purchase what's known these days as the "balanced literacy" or "guided reading" approach, yet another version of the Whole Language approach, still widely embraced, despite its flaws and limited effectiveness. As has been demonstrated for decades, this approach is not effective for the 20 percent of students with dyslexia, who need the structured, explicit, multisensory Orton-Gillingham approach.

Among the more popular reading programs adopted by school districts that are not Orton-Gillingham-based—and thus not effective at teaching children with dyslexia to read, write and spell—are Read 180, System 44, Reading Recovery and Leveled Literacy Intervention. (And there are many more commercial learning and brain training centers that make claims to help dyslexic students with their reading, but do not offer Orton-Gillingham approaches; research them well to make sure they are a good fit for your child's specific needs before investing in them.)

I remember having a conversation about this with a school board member who was trying to comprehend why dyslexic students continued to struggle with a balanced literacy reading program the district purchased. "But we spent well over a million dollars," he lamented, "and we were assured it would work for everyone." It was a program designed for slow learners and English Language Learners, completely ineffective for dyslexic students, which district officials had to admit when parents asked the direct question, yet they continue to use it anyway.

Reading Approaches That Work for Dyslexic Students

Good news: Orton-Gillingham is an approach to teaching reading that works. It requires skilled and experienced educators who provide explicit instruction in a multisensory, structured approach to language that includes phonological awareness, sound-symbol association, syllables, comprehension, grammar, and morphology (the structure of words). In order to learn the approach, educators must commit to extensive study, supervision by a trained practitioner, and practical classroom experience. More good news: Orton-Gillingham training is increasingly available to educators in-person and even online.

As the approach becomes more widely understood and embraced, publishing companies are developing Orton-Gillingham-based programs—even some that come packed up in a nice box complete with its own readers and teaching manuals. Orton-Gillingham based programs that are used by school districts include Barton, Slingerland, Project Read, Lindamood-Bell, Wilson, Nessy, Sonday, Reading Horizons, Take Flight, Read Well, RAVE-O, Toe-by-Toe and more.

Decades ago, students were taught to study the roots, history, structure, and meaning of words as well as how they are built; how suffixes and prefixes affect their meanings, and how to spell them in a predictable and understandable way—according to the rules. Today this is called Structured Word Inquiry or SWI, and it can be a very effective—and fun—way for even very young students to learn what seems to be the secret code of understanding English.

Structured Word Inquiry includes several aspects of learning language including spelling (orthography); the organization of sounds (phonology); the structure and parts of words (morphology) and the history of words and how they change over time (etymology). Phew! The important thing is this approach helps students with dyslexia (and those who aren't dyslexic!) learn to master, manipulate and understand the often-confusing English language.

Trouble with Words

Teachers may call it SSR, which means Silent Sustained Reading. But struggling readers refer to SSR as Sit down, Shut up and Read. Silent reading is just as difficult as reading out loud. For the person with dyslexia, reading a textbook or a novel may look like too many words on a two-page spread, blurring them all together. The spacing may be confusing; the black type against white paper may be disconcerting. Some describe the words as dancing, floating or drifting off the page. Deciphering the squiggles takes an overwhelming effort—so much so that the meaning of the passage frequently gets lost in the process.

The later elementary grades, middle school and high school are all about reading to learn. This slows down the dyslexic student who may understand the subject when presented orally by the teacher, but find it very difficult to do so when reading about it. As a high school freshman explained: "Sometimes I read stuff twice and it doesn't make any sense, and I get confused, I have to concentrate so much on the reading in the textbook, I can't learn what I'm supposed to be learning about. So it takes forever to keep going back and read it again. Then I run out of time and have lots more homework to do."

Also slowing dyslexic readers are letters that all look alike: p, q, d, b are all the same symbol, just positioned differently. Same with m, w, n, u, even 3 and E. Similarly shaped, but differently positioned letters cause no end of confusion for the student with dyslexia working hard to figure out the words.

Simulations can be used to teach parents, teachers and administrators what it's like to experience a classroom with dyslexia. Participating in one—or watching a simulation on YouTube—helps increase understanding of what it's like for students with dyslexia.

The Challenges of "Plain English"

The English language—with its 26 letters and 44 sounds—is filled with confusing exceptions, including multiple sounds for the same letter and silent letters. And rarely are the rules and structure of the language taught explicitly. This presents many difficulties for dyslexic students. Consider these perplexing aspects of English:

* **Homonyms** (words that sound the same and are spelled the same but have different meanings): lying / lying, pen / pen, play / play.
* **Homophones** (words that sound the same but are spelled differently and have different meanings): one / won, do / dew, new / knew, pare / pair / pear, wood / would, throne / thrown, threw / through, rain / reign, council / counsel, blue / blew.
* **Heteronyms:** words that are spelled the same, but sound different: desert / desert; read / read.
* **Words with silent letters or confusing pronunciation:** Autumn, gnome, tongue, simile, pneumonia, bright, epitome, bologna.

Words that *should* sound the same, but don't:

* Good / food
* Bead / head
* Finger / ginger
* How / row
* Cough / slough / dough / rough / plough
* If / of

Words that don't look like they sound the same, but do:

- ✻ Innocents / innocence
- ✻ Independents / independence

Becoming aware of the challenges of the English language is one way to have greater empathy for students who struggle to read—whether they have dyslexia or not!

When making presentations about dyslexia to third- and fourth-graders in classrooms during (dis)Ability Awareness Days, I bring a magnetic board with colorful letters arranged to read: *Wee spel werds eggzaklee az tha soun two uz*. (We spell words exactly as they sound to us.) *Thequ ick br ownf oxju mped ov erth ela zydog*. (The quick brown fox jumped over the lazy dog.) Kids have great fun figuring these out—and increasing their understanding of what it might be like to have the spelling challenges that come with dyslexia.

Workarounds for Working with Words

For students with dyslexia, spelling tests, vocabulary-building exercises and spelling bees are just short of torture. With standardized test prep a prime goal for administrators at every grade level, it's become routine for even kindergartners to take home a list of 20 words a week to master. But no amount of drilling, repetition, or keeping the children in from recess to write words on the board will turn these kids into good spellers. It's not called "drill and kill" for nothing!

Because mere rote memorization doesn't work, a differentiated teaching approach is necessary to reach students with dyslexia. The best way for dyslexic students to add words to their vocabulary is by learning them in context, writing sentences, and figuring out ways to make the obscure and unknown mean something to them.

Access to auditory versions of written material is crucial for dyslexic readers; they can rapidly build their vocabularies by exposure to the words they hear. Children may surprise teachers and even their parents with their command of the spoken language, by using very descriptive and precise words in conversation while at the same time their written work continues to be stilted and limited—in no way as expressive as their speech.

Assistive Technology is a godsend for dyslexic students. Spell check, autocorrect, and many other applications, along with the devices—smartphones, laptops, tablets—to run them are of enormous help for those who have difficulty writing and spelling. New and vastly improved speech-to-text and text-to-speech programs provide ways to put verbal and auditory skills to work in dealing with the written word. Developing familiarity with technology and learning keyboarding skills should be encouraged to help allay spelling frustrations and make written communication more effective.

Even in the digital age, scribing is still a great way to help kids with dyslexia. Children get pretty good at dictating their essays, book reports, and homework assignments to parents who input their words and also see that their offspring are mastering the material.

In school, effective accommodations for students with dyslexia may include writing prompts, reduced word counts for an assignments, building vocabulary based on reading assignments and/or writing words in a sentence rather than by standalone identification. Spelling errors for these students should not affect the grade on class work or homework.

Time-honored, hands-on ways of parents helping students with dyslexia include: reading books aloud, letting your child dictate the sentence, paragraph or essay; working one-on-one on homework assignments. While time-consuming, these methods are very effective.

Writing Challenges and Dysgraphia

Take a look at this passage written by a dyslexic sixth grader:

"The storm at mY house wuz crazy! I was out on my balkiny and the biggest strike lit up the sky and I waz blinded for a minut or tow. Then came the THUUNder my hole houce shook."

It reveals storytelling ability with vivid details and imagery, complete with emphasis on the sound of the thunder, but no understanding of conventional English rules, phonemic awareness, capitalization or spelling. If turned in as a classroom assignment, it would be marked down for multiple errors, likely discouraging any future effort in expressive writing.

Other examples of spelling by the same student, who had been in Special Education for Specific Learning Disability for three years, yet still had not been taught basic rules of the English language: jacit (jacket); famble (family); exsopramint (experiment); SantClos (Santa Claus); Crismus (Christmas); socker (soccer); colieg (college); profeshnel (professional); crentive righting (creative writing); ockword (awkward).

Writing is more than the act of putting pen to paper; it's also the skill of creating sentences, paragraphs, essays and research papers. Students with dyslexia who struggle to read, nearly always struggle to write as well, and to organize their thoughts, ideas, information and knowledge on paper or screen.

A particular curse to dyslexic students is the emphasis, near *obsession*, educators have with the Five Paragraph Essay and its rigid formula: introduction, thesis, three paragraphs with topic sentences and supporting evidence, and a conclusion. Writing in this all left-brain, structured sort of way, and the necessity to squeeze all their thoughts into this small box is a challenge for right-brain dominant children and young adults with dyslexia.

Reading, Writing and Arithmetic

When students with dyslexia aren't taught properly how to read or the rules of English, they have an added burden when it comes to writing—and rarely receive appropriate instruction in that academic skill either. A student may have great understanding of a subject, and be able to discuss it, or present mastery of it in many ways, but writing is certainly not the best way.

Dysgraphia, difficulty in writing, results in atrocious penmanship that's surprisingly similar in style from one person to another. It may be due to poor small-motor skills or caused by processing differences that create a disorientation, making it difficult to form letters, sentences and paragraphs on the page. Poorly formed letters are all jammed together with too few spaces; capitals may appear for no particular reason. Spelling is best and, most kindly, termed creative.

Assistive technology is a blessing, keyboarding an important skill, and yet there is still much to be said for children putting pen to paper and learning to print—and to write cursive. Writing cursive allows the flow of one letter to another, and provides a sensory engagement that is important to children with dyslexia—who often have poor penmanship.

Unfortunately for students with dyslexia, Common Core standards do not include the teaching of cursive, and its instruction is not as widespread as it once was. Convincing evidence suggests that writing in cursive is beneficial in many ways: it helps with fine motor control because it has a flow, and it's not so stop-and-start as making every letter in print; it helps with more uniform spacing and size of letters; each letter is more distinct, so reversals are not as common; it helps the student recognize the breaks between words and where each letter begins on the line.

Project-Based Learning

A much better way for students with dyslexia to demonstrate knowledge of a subject is by creating an individual project or by working with other students to create a group project.

This can be a collaborative approach to learning, using big-picture thinking and solving real-world issues. And it can also be a way for a student who struggles to write to communicate knowledge in another way. Consider the possibility of working with teachers to create project-based alternative ways of assessing knowledge by encouraging dyslexic students to express their interests and show alternate skills by:

* Creating a video
* Making a timeline
* Assembling a photo-journal or a diary
* Putting together a mobile or a diorama

Instead of writing a book report, students can dress up like the author or a character.

One mother told of how her dyslexic daughter had great difficulty writing an essay about the family traditions of *Dia de Los Muertos*, but created a complex three-dimensional altar that skillfully demonstrated her understanding of the significance and meaning of the holiday.

Using the iPad, my son created an amazing slide show of the Civil Rights Movement and set it to "We Shall Overcome." The iPad allowed him to demonstrate his knowledge in a creative way that worked for him, when writing an essay would have been an arduous experience that would not have revealed his in-depth understanding of the struggle for freedom by African-Americans. (Famed dyslexic and iPad creator Steve Jobs knew exactly how to create the tactile, visual and revolutionary Apple innovations for students who have a different way of thinking—and learning—just like he did.)

Class Notes

Taking notes in class during a lecture can be challenging for a student with dyslexia. It requires the multitasking skills of focusing on what's being said, figuring out how to pick out the most important points, and writing legibly enough to be read later—way too much to process simultaneously,

Students with dyslexia learn best by listening to the lecture in class and obtaining notes afterward from a note-taker or the teacher. Another strategy is to tape a lecture and listen to it later—everything from a smart phone to a special pen has recording capability these days. (Note: Students should obtain permission from their teachers before any recording takes place.)

Copying assignments from the board, long an issue for students with dyslexia, is easy these days. A quick click of the smart phone, and a photo of the material is easily available for future reference.

Arithmetic and Dyscalculia

Dyscalculia, "trouble with numbers," is another misunderstood learning difference. The difficulty students have in making sense of what the numbers and arithmetic symbols represent is not much different from those with dyslexia understanding the written word.

The student who has a combination of dyslexia, dysgraphia and dyscalculia, may experience great challenges coping in the traditional classroom, since one issue compounds the other. Difficulty reading means word problems in math class are virtually impossible to decipher. Difficulty writing letters and numbers means calculations may be correct, but not understood by the person who grades the work. Repeated failure creates repeated failure.

When children struggle in math class, it's imperative to get them assessed and pinpoint the difficulties. Remediation can only occur from an appropriate baseline, and an understanding of the student's needs. Too often students are moved along from grade to grade, goals are set and never met, and they reach high school with little understanding of basic mathematical functions. When they hit pre-algebra, then algebra and geometry, the gaps in their knowledge become painfully obvious.

Students with dyscalculia can learn to do math—often at an extraordinarily high level—but similar to those with dyslexia who must be taught to read differently, so, too, do these students require a different approach. Strategies include multi-sensory, concrete techniques such as 3D models and manipulatives; use of pictures and diagrams, such as the number line; use of fingers, calculators and scratch paper; providing formulas during tests. For older students with dyscalculia, intensive intervention and remediation services are required to get them up to grade level.

Students may also rush through their work, causing additional errors. They may misread the function signs, or may have a hard time keeping their calculations neat and organized in order to perform the work. And they may be overwhelmed with the sheer amount of homework expected; all these difficulties can be anticipated and accommodated in the classroom.

8

Dyslexia and Special Education

Students with dyslexia rarely belong in Special Education. If they are identified early and taught how to read in the way they learn, and their learning differences are accommodated in the classroom, they shouldn't need the remediation or "pullout services" offered in Special Education.

Students with dyslexia are too often placed in Special Education because administrators have no other place to provide them with individual attention or an appropriate educational approach.

The path to Special Education for most students with dyslexia goes something like this: Janey and Johnny, originally excited about going to kindergarten, soon find themselves shriveling in the classroom, unable to keep up with their peers in reading, writing and spelling. Their early enthusiasm about learning turns to dread by third grade when they're still struggling to read.

At long last, mom, dad, or a concerned teacher, intervenes and insists Janey and Johnny get "tested," are found to have "Specific Learning Disability," and thus qualified for Special Education services. The word dyslexia will likely not be used in any school discussions.

Once in Special Education, Janey and Johnny may get "pullout services," meaning they will be pulled out from their general education classes for resource classes. In Special Ed, they may receive reading instruction developed for "slow" readers, or for English language learners. It's highly unlikely they will receive the multi-sensory reading approach such as Orton-Gillingham they really need.

As their unaddressed reading deficits increase as they grow older, they will be placed in low-level general education courses, and perhaps, instructional classes through Special Education—despite their intelligence and ability to learn at a high level. The gap between their intellectual potential and the quality of teachers and classes they're allowed to attend will get wider and wider. They will miss out on learning how to use their capacity for reasoning and their unique creative ability to think outside the box.

They will have difficulty taking notes in class, and completing their reading and writing assignments outside of class. With low reading and writing skills, and high levels of frustration, only 78 percent of Special Education students nationwide earn a high school diploma. Janey and Johnny no longer have much hope of planning for higher education because they haven't had the appropriate course of study and have begun to believe they are not smart enough to go to college. They probably won't be steered to take high-level classes, or fulfill the requirements to apply to college. If they are lucky they won't go off-track with behavioral, self-esteem or substance abuse issues.

Exams will not reflect their intelligence, potential or understanding of the material and, as a result, neither will their GPAs or their scores on the ACT or SAT.

They may drum up the courage to attend the local community college, where they will likely be required to take remedial courses because their K-12 education did not prepare them for college level work. This can be very discouraging, unless they register for supportive services and develop the confidence to self-advocate for accommodations with every professor. If they obtain appropriate accommodations and assistive technology solutions, they may, for the first time, excel in their studies and realize their full academic potential.

Special Ed Zone: DyslexiaLand's Most Challenging Place

As long as educators continue the practice of placing students with dyslexia in Special Ed, parents will be compelled to lead their children through the Special Education Zone, the most challenging and dangerous of all territories to travel in DyslexiaLand.

Most parents are surprised to learn that school officials do not "diagnose" dyslexia (or any other disability);

rather, they determine whether the student qualifies for Special Education services based on testing results.

School districts resist using the word "dyslexia," because with identification of dyslexia comes the necessity of offering a proven program that teaches students with dyslexia in the way they learn. But dyslexia advocates and federal guidelines advise otherwise. Precise language matters, and parents should use the word as much as possible in conversation and correspondence.

School officials will often say that a student qualifies for Special Education services under the term "Specific Learning Disability." Parents are confused by this terminology for good reason: virtually no one outside of Special Education departments has ever heard of Specific Learning Disability! Many parents have spent countless hours trying to figure what all this SLD stuff is all about.

It all gets more complicated when school officials attempt to make a distinction between such issues as "auditory processing" "working memory," "rapid naming," and "phonological processing," particularly if they are not equipped or prepared to deliver services to address each unique issue, which is usually the case.

Semantics aside, what can you do if your child qualifies for Special Education services? Do you even want them?

The Individualized Education Program (IEP)

If you choose the Special Education route, you will have the opportunity to work with a team at your child's school, meet to go over all the testing results, and together determine the way forward. Your child may qualify for an "Individualized Education Program (IEP)," which will provide for educational goals, with specialized instruction and classroom accommodations to help achieve them. This is part of your child's right to the "Fair Appropriate Public Education (FAPE)," as guaranteed by Federal law under the Individuals with Disabilities Education Act (IDEA).

Remember that the "I" in "IEP" is "Individualized." I hope that you never attend an IEP, as I have, where the principal directs the Special Education staffer to prepare a "boilerplate IEP," or when there is no draft IEP document developed, and parents are simply told that the Special Education teacher will come up with a list of goals for you to sign off on.

An IEP meeting is supposed to be an opportunity for the assembled team to decide on the best approaches to take in the best interests of the child. Goals drafted for the IEP should be specific and measurable. They should use action words, and be realistic, relevant, and time-limited.

As an equal member of the Special Education IEP team (that may include a school psychologist, administrator, or specialized service providers such as a speech therapist), you must speak up, sharing knowledge about best practices to help students with dyslexia in general and your child's learning style and classroom needs in particular. It is up to you to monitor your child's progress and call an IEP meeting when necessary.

The 504 Plan

Another way to support your child with classroom accommodations is with a "504 Plan," which is governed under the Americans with Disabilities Act (ADA) and ensures nondiscrimination for individuals with a disability (and for these purposes dyslexia is considered a disability). It is enforced through the Office of Civil Rights, a sub agency of the U.S. Department of Education. A 504 may or may not include specialized instruction, and may allow accommodations like extra time to complete assignments, alternative setting for testing, preferential seating, and the use of assistive technology.

Some parents of students with dyslexia opt for a 504 to obtain accommodations, and avoid the Special Education services altogether, while seeking appropriate reading instruction outside the school setting. For a discussion of the difference between an IEP and a 504 Plan, and all other legal matters related to Special Education, consult Wrightslaw: wrightslaw.com.

"Qualifying" for Special Education

Parents of students with dyslexia can be shocked, surprised, and confused when they learn that their child qualifies for Special Education services. Those unfamiliar with the world of Special Education may think that it's solely intended for students who have cognitive impairment, major behavior or emotional issues, or physical challenges.

No less than 13 categories of disabilities qualify students for Special Ed. They are: autism, blindness, deafness, emotional disturbance, hearing impairment, intellectual disability, multiple disabilities, orthopedic impairment, other health impaired, specific learning disability, speech or language impairment, traumatic brain injury, and visual impairment.

Within Special Education, a distinction is made between disabilities that are mild-moderate and those that are moderate-severe. Students with dyslexia are nearly always in the category of mild-moderate, and require very different services than those in moderate-severe.

By far the highest percentage of students who qualify for Special Education are classified as mild-moderate with Specific Learning Disability—approximately 60 percent. Of that 60 percent, approximately 80 percent have dyslexia.

Parents of children with mild-moderate issues rarely share the same concerns as those whose children have moderate-severe ones. This leads to many misunderstandings about the purpose of Special Education, and often a sense of embarrassment for kids who "just have dyslexia" about being in Special Education. Other students and even general education teachers may view "SPED Kids" as a label that means students receiving those services—including those with dyslexia—have limited intellectual potential.

In these days of inclusion, educators repeat a mantra about Special Education as a service, not a place. The notion is that Special Education instruction and accommodations can be delivered in the general education classroom; however, that's not always understood, much less carried out. Ideally, general education and Special Education departments understand each other's needs and collaborate effectively, but there's often a disconnect between them. Providing appropriate services often falls to general education teachers who may not have much knowledge of—or interest in—dyslexia and how to meet the needs of dyslexic students.

On most campuses, there is a "Special Education Room" that may be known as the Learning Center, or the Resource Room, but everyone knows what it is—and who goes there. When my son was in elementary school, every day he went to the Learning Center located in a portable trailer for Special Education. And when he was in high school, everyone knew that Room 108 was the Special Education Room.

Adding to the negative perception of Special Ed are the parents, community members and educators who claim that Special Education services are a drain of tax-payer funds, a joke, a scam, a waste of money, and a way to deprive "regular" or "gifted" kids of their education.

Not every student with dyslexia qualifies for Special Education services—even those who have undergone comprehensive examination and even diagnosis by a professional neuropsychologist. The school district must consider, but won't always accept those results. Sometimes assessments done by school personnel do not detect dyslexia—and services will be denied, even if recommended by a private consultant.

Who's in Special Education, Who's Not, and Why

With students with dyslexia comprising 20 percent of the population, and only around 12 percent of all children enrolled in school receiving Special Education services, it's easy to calculate that a majority of kids with dyslexia are not identified as such, and likely are struggling in the general education population. If Special Education typically is the only way students with dyslexia gain access to individualized instruction, obviously a lot of them are being skipped and missed!

Reasons for this oversight abound: parents may choose to deal with dyslexia outside of the school setting; the district may lack proper educational approaches for dyslexia; some students with dyslexia do not qualify due to legal definitions and testing criteria.

If you're unsure about whether or not to put your child into Special Education, check with your local school district to discover the success of its Special Education program. The district should have reports about such factors as graduation rate, percentage of students in AP classes; percentage of students accepted at 4-year colleges, as well as the truancy, dropout and expulsion rates. You might be pleasantly surprised by the numbers, or may be absolutely horrified to discover results that are terribly low in academic areas, and so very high in the disciplinary ones. Make your decisions accordingly.

Some years back, a management team was hired by my school district to analyze the ineffective Special Education department. The lead consultant offered what he termed a "scathing" and "brutal" indictment, observing: "Students come into this district with learning disabilities, and they leave with emotional disturbances."

It may be the case that you live in a school district that offers excellent services for dyslexic students. A growing number of school districts with an enlightened administration are insisting on improved teacher training and providing appropriate services for students. And there are an increasing number of public charter school academies that are designed for students with dyslexia.

It's what we all want—quality services for students, well-trained educators delighted to share their expertise as they teach your child, and compassionate administrators who are determined to make a positive difference. If that is the case, appreciate the educators and the system that created them—and sing their praises far and wide! As parents who advocate effectively influence other parents, so, too, do educators and school districts that address dyslexia effectively influence their colleagues elsewhere.

Requesting Testing

In order for their child to be considered for Special Education services, parents must make a request for testing in writing.

Well-intentioned parents think they are requesting Special Education assessment when they say to an educator, "I would like to have my child tested for dyslexia." That request typically elicits a response like this one: "We don't test for dyslexia. You have to have that done privately." So the parents walk away, puzzled, and, if they have the means, may shell out thousands of dollars for a private assessment. Or they may feel stymied by that turndown and throw up their hands.

The educator's response should have been informative, respectful and understanding, something like: "*Please talk to me about your concerns and what leads you to request an assessment for your child, which we most certainly can do. You need to know, however, that the school system does not diagnose through its testing, but it does conduct adequate testing to determine whether or not your child qualifies for Special Education services. Is this a good time for us to talk, or would you like to schedule an appointment?"*

You must make your request for an assessment for all suspected disabilities in writing, which starts the clock (mandated response time varies by school district and state) for the district to respond to you with an assessment plan. Date all correspondence and keep copies. In DyslexiaLand in general, and with IEPs in particular, paperwork reigns supreme and piles up alarmingly quickly.

The IEP Meeting

What is supposed to be a meeting of the minds of team members on behalf of a child can turn into a minefield of misunderstanding, miscommunication and stress like nothing else a parent experiences.

It's usually held in a classroom or a "Learning Center," where students receive Special Education services. What that means in reality is that parents of elementary school students are often seated in tiny little chairs meant for children, scrunched submissively in these perches, while the educator in charge sits in a big, comfortable teacher's chair. Or the meeting may be held in a large Special Education room at a huge table filled with school district employees.

Typically—and depending on the age and needs of the child—the members of the team who are invited to attend include the parents, the principal of the school or other administrator, the Special Education specialist, a general education teacher, a district administrator, an educational psychologist, and any number of specialists who might be called in, such as a speech and language pathologist or mental health specialist. If the parents bring an attorney, the district brings one, too. If the parents want the meeting recorded, they must make their request in advance. If approved, they can record it and the district will record it, too.

The meeting begins with the sign-in of all parties present, and the presentation of rights to the parents—a multi-page legal-ese document that spells out your rights and the district's obligations. (I've always wondered what would happen if I said to school officials, "I'd like to read this document aloud before we begin." Ha!) But seriously, the document is very important, and you should take the time to read it and familiarize yourself with its contents.

When an assessment team convenes to evaluate and report the results of testing a child for learning disabilities, the initial experience can be overwhelmingly stressful and negative for the parents hearing the news. The annual IEP meeting, and the triennial meeting—which goes over more testing—are equally stressful experiences for most parents.

Before these meetings take place, you may be requested to fill out one or more questionnaires about your child's behaviors. Your assessment may be altogether different from what the educators report.

These meetings are typically conducted in a language common to Special Educators, in a jargon that's frequently off-putting and incomprehensible to parents, who may experience the IEP as cold, clinical and without compassion. When test results are examined in excruciating detail, it can feel as though the child is reduced to a set of numbers that zigzagged across the normal, average range, landing on very high and very low scores—leaving parents devastated, frightened for their child's future, and frustrated about what to do.

When goals are set for the child, school officials are loathe to provide specific strategies for accomplishing them, and discussions about accommodations might be left to the parent—rather than the staff—to suggest them, so prepare well in advance of the meeting.

It's often a rough experience for even the most seasoned parent; one that requires preparation and a steely resolve to get the school officials to do their jobs and follow the law. Parents are advised to bring a knowledgeable friend or advocate for support, someone who can take notes, and offer another perspective to the proceedings.

Keep your cool and remember that you can wait to sign the document until it is complete with all the notes and new goals included—and you have an agreement.

Tips for the IEP Meeting

Bring snacks. Some parents feel compelled to bring treats to an IEP meeting—bottles of water, cookies, fruit or trail mix. It's not necessary, but is a nice idea, and may help set a tone—or at the very least keep energy flowing during a long meeting.

Be prepared. Request all documents in advance so that you can review them at your leisure and be prepared to discuss them during the IEP meeting.

Express your concerns. During the meeting, there is a time to discuss "parental concerns." Be sure to consider them in advance, and fully express them during the meeting.

Personalize it. Since many of the education professionals attending the meeting will know your child only by the statistics and descriptions on paper, humanize the situation. Bring a photograph of your child as a reminder of what the process is all about. You may also want to bring in a writing sample, or an audio or video recording of your child reading aloud, or of your child describing what it's like to struggle with classwork.

Student participation. Think about at what age you want your child to participate in an IEP meeting. High school students should be informed and involved as much as possible so that they can understand their needs, effectively self-advocate in their classes, and prepare for their college years. But depending on the subject matter at hand, you may decide that they do not need to be in all the meetings, particularly if it would add to anxiety or damage self-esteem.

Supreme Court Support

In the 2017 case of Endrew F. v. Douglas County (Colorado) School District, the Supreme Court justices unanimously determined that IDEA requires more than a minimal year-to-year progress, and that goals for an IEP "must be appropriately ambitious in light of (a child's) circumstances, just as advancement from grade to grade is appropriately ambitious for most children in the regular classroom."

This decision aids parents who may be frustrated by the often low expectations of Special Education simply providing "some benefit," as Chief Justice John Roberts wrote, "When all is said and done, a student offered an educational program providing 'merely more than de minimis' progress from year to year can hardly be said to have been offered an education at all."

Keep this in mind when setting IEP goals, and use the acronym SMART to remember that they should be Specific, Measurable, Actionable, Realistic and Timely.

Special Education Insider Tips

There's a lot that "they" won't tell you, and you have to learn on your own, Here's a short course for what parents need to know about and what they may encounter in the twists and turns in the world of Special Education.

Ask for accommodations. 504 or IEP teams are rarely proactive in exploring or proposing a wide range of accommodations that would be appropriate or desirable for your child. Usually such teams offer only the most obvious accommodations, without individualizing them. The list is pretty predictable, including extra time on homework and tests and preferential seating.

You may request additional accommodations, such as alternate testing locations, for weekly student/teacher meetings to go over homework verbally (rather than writing out worksheets in order to show understanding and mastery of the material), or teachers not lowering grades for spelling. Talk with your child to get a clear picture of what might work, such as a limited number of math problems on a page or additional time on assignments.

Put it in writing. Know that in Special Education, *if it isn't written down, it didn't happen*. That goes for during the IEP meeting, or for any meeting, phone calls or hallway conversations you might have with staff. *Put it in writing*. This is an absolute necessity.

Email dominance. One of the techniques employed by some educators when they want to convey information, but not take ownership over it, is to push for a phone call or an informal meeting, but not an email; this leaves no trace that the conversation ever took place. Always take complete notes during any phone call or meeting, particularly an IEP, so that you have a record of what transpired. Protect yourself by always writing a follow-up email to record and summarize a conversation, meeting, or other encounter.

Parents send long, detailed, even impassioned emails to communicate with a teacher, school district official or even a school board member, and then are disappointed when they get no reply or the reply is terse, circumspect, or less-than-complete.

A "no reply" from a school official to your email might be for the same reasons senders get "no reply" to emails sent in the business world: The receiver gets too many emails, the sender didn't ask for immediate action, the sender asked for too many things, the email was too long, what you have to say isn't important to the recipient, or there just isn't any benefit to the recipient in responding to you. When school officials respond in the most brief manner possible, it might be because they regard your email as something that may hold them accountable later, or even as a legal document.

School officials often do not reply directly to the email, but instead start a new e-mail with a different subject heading in order to avoid answering direct questions, addressing only what they want to, and ignoring the rest. It's a way to lose information and it sometimes seems as though district officials regard every word written back to parents as potential incriminating evidence against them were parents to file suit. This obfuscating email practice makes it a challenge for parents to keep track of a single subject, and adds to the amount of paperwork and what may already be difficult and tense communication. You may choose to print out correspondence as it occurs so that you have a complete written record of it.

Wait to fail. Unwritten policies (enforced nevertheless by many principals) encourage parents to wait before having their children assessed. Schools routinely declare that it's their policy not to test students until third grade. Just think of how far behind their peers these students will find themselves when subjected to these "wait and see" approaches. Many times classroom teachers *know* a child needs additional assessments but fear for their positions if they refer too many students, or advocate too strongly for more training, or for more classroom assistance for poor readers.

Know that Child Find is part of the federal IDEA and requires schools to identify students who may have a disability, and who may need additional services, and refer them for evaluation.

Principals may put parents off by saying that they should just wait until the student moves on to the next school; or takes the state standardized testing in the spring, before proceeding with any Special Education assessments. Assessments have nothing whatsoever to do with standardized testing, and it's completely inappropriate for a principal or any other educator to link them or to make such a recommendation.

Messing with the testing. Watch out for the trickery that includes selective or incomplete testing: Not bothering to test for phonological processing, or administering only portions of a test. Beware, too of what a state-level educational consultant termed the "Las Vegas Approach to Testing." In this, the assessor administers a test for current reading levels, then "bets" (after reviewing the results that showed a downturn in performance) that the student wasn't trying hard enough, and administers the exact same test a few days later. Hard to tell what results would be accurate and valid with that one! The purpose of this gamble is to see if a student with dyslexia can score sufficiently high on one of the tests to not qualify for Special Education services.

Going down the rabbit hole. Educators have been known to drag things out, convening endless numbers of meetings to discuss one aspect of the student's education, or another. These educators are well paid, and have none of the urgency of parents to address a student's issues. As part of their regular workday, they can schedule numerous meetings—and space them out over time—to revisit the same subject again and again and again, while most parents have to take off work in order to attend these meetings. For parents, quantity of meetings is no substitute for quality: a half-dozen meetings, each one featuring a different cast of educators, sometimes only in attendance by phone, is an ineffective approach to say the least.

Meetings drag on and on with little new ground covered, when new members are added to the group and must brought up to speed. This burns up precious time—and goodwill. Meanwhile your boss wonders why you're so stressed out and taking so much time off work to attend school meetings for your child.

Intimidation and bullying. Never underestimate a bureaucrat's inclination to wield an overblown sense of power over you, your child, indeed your entire family. Case in point: A concerned mother I know requested assessment for her high school student (who had previously qualified for Special Education). Within two days the assistant principal had assembled a Student Study Team, complete with classroom teacher, counselor, Special Education teachers, and invited the parents and son to attend.

At the meeting, educators made negative comments about the student being unmotivated and having a bad attitude, tried to discourage the idea of testing because it would take 10 to 20 hours, and suggested that the student consider attending an out-of-town military boarding school for high-risk students run by the National Guard.

Naturally, this family was rattled when their earnest request for an assessment for processing issues turned into something so negative. The son felt betrayed by his parents, while the parents felt betrayed by the system. The whole episode was made worse when one of the educators mocked the student's passion for cross-country running. "What happens if you get hit by a car?" he asked the boy. With brutal irony, two weeks later, the boy was hit by a car, sustaining broken bones and a traumatic brain injury—and taking his life into a completely different direction, and needing even more Special Education services and accommodations than ever.

Bullying is common in the IEP process, when parents may be outnumbered by educators in a meeting by a margin of 6 to 1, or 10 to 2. Often parents are strongly "requested" to sign the IEP at the end of the meeting, even if the document is not complete with the notes, team decisions, or accommodations discussed at the meeting.

Confidential settlements. One way districts deal with parent demands for services without changing the way they do business as usual is to make an offer for a confidential settlement agreement. Much goes on behind closed doors in a school district, and expenditures are made that are never known by parents of students or by the taxpaying public.

School officials may grant quality remedial services outside the school setting for one child at a time, but due to these non-disclosure agreements, the child's parents are prevented from communicating the good news or helping other parents whose children would benefit from the same top-tier services.

Swimming in denial. Educators might make parents feel like they've brought an unusual problem into their lives, with a comment like, "Well, I've never had a student with dyslexia before; you'll have to teach me what to do." Guaranteed, they have, they just didn't know—or didn't bother to address it appropriately. Others blame the students, with comments about their lack of motivation, interest or effort. Or they may insist that secondary negative behaviors or attention issues are of primary concern, ignoring the possibility that they are secondary to unidentified and unaddressed learning issues.

This lack of properly trained teachers puts a major burden on school districts to provide professional development for their staff members. It may not be the fault of the individual teacher, but it is a source of contention, when parents realize that a teacher needs on-the-job training in order to teach their child to read, or to implement appropriate accommodations.

Sometimes the teacher will rely on administrators to make the competency case with comments like, "Well you know, she is a credentialed teacher" (even though the credentialing program didn't include one minute of training about dyslexia). Or, "Yes, I do think that watching an hour-long video on YouTube is sufficient Orton-Gillingham training to teach your child to read." Or worst of all: "No, we do not think that your child is at a disadvantage because he is the first student this teacher is working with in this new program. After all, someone has to be the first, and we don't consider this on-the-job-training."

And how about this whopper? "I have to trust my teachers when they say they can do something; let's give her two months working with your child, and then re-evaluate."

Sometimes education personnel—who should know better—pretend they know nothing about dyslexia. They may argue about what to call it; they may send you to your pediatrician for a diagnosis. They may claim dyslexia is not a part of the state education code; they may quibble over the percentage of students who have dyslexia; they may try to foist off a computer program or alternative reading program that isn't intended for students with dyslexia, or they may institute pilot programs for a handful of students taught by unqualified educators, and pretend they have a scalable model. Recognize these approaches for that they are: stalling and diversionary tactics that do nothing to help your child with dyslexia.

Special Education Action Plan

1) **Communicate** your concerns to your child's classroom teacher.
2) **Cooperate** with the suggestions made by educators, but keep an acceptable timeline in mind.
3) **Intervention** begins typically as Student Study Team or the Response to Intervention (RTI). Do not allow this to turn into a time-consuming way to keep your child from receiving appropriate services.

4) **Implement a follow-up plan.** If, after the agreed-upon time your child is not making sufficient progress, be firm and persistent about obtaining additional help.

5) **Make a written request** for an assessment for all suspected disabilities. Too often parents simply express their concern to a teacher, and are waved away with assurances. If you are truly concerned, write a letter to the principal of the school to request the beginning of an assessment process, stating your concerns about your child's issues in school. This is the entry point to the process of determining whether or not Special Education services are appropriate.

6) **Obtain appropriate classroom accommodations** for your child. Even when they learn to read at grade level, students with dyslexia will typically need additional time, access to notes, and access to auditory or visual information (eg. downloadable books or movie versions of books). Project-based assessments, reduced homework load, overlooking spelling and grammatical errors, and oral exams rather than written ones may be encouraged.

7) **Keep impeccable records.** If your struggling child is found to be eligible for Special Education services, you will be entering a bureaucratic world filled with gatekeepers who speak a strange language and who move around mountains of paperwork. Stay on top of the paperwork as you receive it and it won't

overwhelm you. Keep it organized by school year in a binder or a file box.

8) **Maintain good relationships** with teachers, administrators, and even school board members to ensure that the needs of students with dyslexia are addressed appropriately. Let them know that you appreciate their efforts when they meet or communicate with you, or make an overture that assists you or the dyslexic community.

9) **Make the commitment: Do whatever you have to do.** A student with dyslexia needs parental intervention to make sure to stay on the pathway to success—and it's a long journey. That student may need extra help with homework; may need to be read to; may need a parent to act as a scribe; will likely need extra help developing organizational skills—and yes—may need specialized tutoring services if the school simply is not helping. Know when to cut your losses and get the help your child needs. Do what needs to be done, and keep going—all the way through school.

10) **Appreciate your child's extra efforts.** Virtually every student with dyslexia works harder for less (immediately obvious) reward than other students. That perseverance and determination may pay off significantly later in life. Let your child—and educators—know that you are aware that this extra work

builds character and determination, even if it doesn't seem to do so in the moment.

Speaking Their Language: Acronyms in SPED (Special Education)

In DyslexiaLand in general, and in the Special Ed Zone in particular, additional communication problems arise from the maddening use of acronyms by school officials, who literally speak a different language when they use them as words.

Communication can come to a halt when they invoke them; parents should always ask for clarification if this happens.

As you read through the information and paperwork to find ways to help your child with dyslexia, you'll encounter many acronyms and abbreviations. If you're not sure how to decipher this alphabet soup, it's difficult to fully understand what educators are telling you. So to assist you with the translation process, here are common acronyms and the words they represent.

Acronyms

2E: Twice Exceptional

504: Section 504 Plan of the Rehabilitation Act of 1973

ACT: American College Testing

ADD: Attention Deficit Disorder

ADA: American Disabilities Act

ADHD: Attention Deficit Hyperactivity Disorder

AET: Association of Educational Therapists

APD: Auditory Processing Disorder

ASL: American Sign Language

AT: Assistive Technology

AYP: Adequate Yearly Progress

BIP: Behavior Intervention Plan

BOE: Board of Education

CCSS: Common Core State Standards

CTOPP-2: Comprehensive Test of Phonological Processing, 2nd edition

DIBELS: Dynamic Indicators of Basic Early Literacy Skills

DSM 5: Diagnostic and Statistical Manual of Mental Disorders

ECE: Early Childhood Education

ELL: English Language Learner

ESL: English as a Second Language

ESSA: Every Child Succeeds Act

ESY: Extended School Year

ETS: Educational Testing Service

FAPE: Free Appropriate Public Education

FCMAT: Fiscal Crisis Management Team

FERPA: Family Educational Rights and Privacy Act

FMRI: Functional Magnetic Resonance Imaging

FOIA: Freedom of Information Act

GATE: Gifted and Talented Education

GE: General Education

GSLN: Gifted Student with Learning Needs

Dyslexia and Special Education

IDEA: Individuals with Disabilities Education Act

IEE: Independent Educational Evaluation

IEP: Individual Education Program

IQ: Intelligence Quotient

ITP: Individual Transition Plan

LEA: Local Educational Agency

LRE: Least Restrictive Environment

MOU: Memorandum of Understanding

MSLE: Multisensory Structured Language Education

NCLB: No Child Left Behind

OCR: Office of Civil Rights

OG: Orton-Gillingham

OHI: Other Health Impairment

OT: Occupational Therapy

PLEP: Present Level of Educational Performance

PP: Paraprofessional

RTI: Response to Intervention

SAT: Scholastic Aptitude Test

SEA: State Education Agency

SELPA: Special Education Local Plan Area

SI: Sensory Integration

SLD: Specific Learning Disability

SLI: Specific Language Impairment

SLP: Speech and Language Program

SPED: Special Education

SST: Student Study Team

UDL: Universal Design for Learning

USD: Unified School District

USDOE: United States Department of Education

VAKT: Visual, Auditory, Kinesthetic and Tactile learning styles

WIA: Workforce Investment Act

WISC: Wechsler Intelligence Scale for Children

WJ4: Woodcock-Johnson Psycho-educational Battery

9

Advocating for Your Child

Until the school system can be trusted to treat students with dyslexia appropriately—academically and emotionally—it is incumbent upon a parent to protect their child, and take a strong interest in their life—at school and beyond.

You must do some soul-searching and determine for yourself how to work with educators to deliver the legal protections due your child, while at the same time building your child's understanding, skills and abilities to deal with the challenges of dyslexia. And you must be aware that many parents-turned-advocates worry about retaliation. School officials will always deny that retaliation against parents—and their children—occurs, but it does. Pay attention, document all actions and, as much as possible, work at keeping emotion out of dealing with the schools.

As the parent advocating for a dyslexic child, you may encounter derisive comments from educators, even from other parents, that you are a "helicopter parent," doing too much to intervene in school.

The definition of a "helicopter parent" is one who "takes an overprotective or excessive interest in the life of their child." There's a lot that's subject to interpretation with that description, and parents will have to sort out for themselves what is "overprotective" or "excessive."

Much is said these days about "grit" and "resilience" as essential qualities for success. I maintain that dyslexic children develop those skills far beyond non-dyslexic children because the very nature of their learning differences requires persistence and determination, figuring out workarounds, and overcoming repeated setbacks in school.

Parents' insistence that their IEPs, 504s and accommodations be enforced, and that their children have the opportunity to participate in classes and extra-curricular activities in which they excel will not prevent them from developing "grit" or "resilience." Instead, it will simply level the playing field and ensure that the dyslexic student gets a fair chance to succeed—without repeatedly experiencing the soul-crushing failures that are all-too-familiar to generations of dyslexic individuals.

In general, it's my parenting style, and advocacy position, to offer students more positives and fewer negatives—more carrot and less stick—in order to maximize their chances to develop without being defeated. Along the way, it's important to teach children self-advocacy skills. Realistically, however, they are not likely to be emotionally or psychologically equipped to do much effective self-advocacy until they enter their late teens, after years of explicit instruction and support. Until that time, they need their parents to lead the way and protect them from a system not made for them.

Beware of the "Wait to Fail" Approach

Parents expect their children to succeed in school, especially those are bright, motivated and excited about learning. *So When Things Go Wrong*, there's a tendency to reach for every lifeline offered. Parents want to believe those common reassurances offered by teachers and administrators: "Your child will grow out of it." "Your child will learn to focus." "Your child just needs to be more motivated and work harder."

Don't believe those platitudes.

Comforting as they may be in the moment, these canned responses serve only to delay identification of dyslexia, as well as the introduction of timely interventions and individualized instructional approaches necessary for these children to move forward. Abundant research suggests that a child who experiences difficulties reading—without appropriate interventions—will grow into an adult who experiences difficulties reading. "Wait to Fail" is an unconscionable approach and there's really no time at all to waste to identify why a child unexpectedly struggles in school.

Parents must realize early that it is a mistake to wait to intervene when a child is struggling or think that added maturity or a change in attitude might help a student learn to read, write and spell.

Why Educators Can't and Often Don't Help Dyslexic Students

Parents are often baffled when classroom teachers and administrators, who previously had been ever-so-pleasant to them suddenly get testy, defensive, even hostile, when parents press them about reading issues. Parents will encounter resistance to teaching children with dyslexia in the way they learn in the form of system-wide dysfunction and from:

Educators who don't know how to help dyslexic students, and avoid, cover-up or pretend otherwise. They will try piecemeal solutions and reassure parents: "Don't worry, it will get better next year."

Educators who know how to help dyslexic students but can't provide it, because the necessary programs and personnel are unavailable or because district policies prevent them from using best practices.

Educators who know what dyslexic students need and try with limited success to provide it. For example, an Orton-Gillingham program might be available but the one-on-one instruction necessary to teach it can't be implemented due to school policies and budget issues. Like one well-trained Orton-Gillingham specialist noted: "I can do my best teaching practices, but in a group setting with six kids, I don't think it's going to do any of these children much good."

Become an Advocate

"What will happen to my child?" That nagging question gets louder and louder as more time passes, student failures increase, and parent concerns multiply.

When parents realize that the public school can't or won't teach their dyslexic child, they must take action. Quickly.

Teachers may *like* children, but they don't *love* them in the way parents do.

Parents know their child's temperament, know their strengths and challenges, know their child's different learning style, and what works and what doesn't.

It's up to parents to lead their children through DyslexiaLand. As the Hopi say: "We are the ones we've been waiting for."

Parents just starting out may not know what they don't know about advocacy, but they have more ways to find out than every before. Many who have already passed this way are willing to help others get on the right path.

Look for support from Decoding Dyslexia, a strong grassroots movement of parents from across the nation to learn, teach and advocate for change. With a motto of "Educate. Advocate. Legislate." and a presence in every state, Decoding Dyslexia offers sponsored events, info-packed websites, and lively Facebook pages. Parents can share information, insights and advice almost instantaneously with parents located faraway.

No one is a better researcher than a parent on a mission to help a struggling child; with so much information and many resources now readily available, it's not uncommon for parents to rapidly become more knowledgeable about dyslexia than educators and administrators.

When parents with a strong commitment to their children and with solid grounding in their own "dyslexia education" begin to advocate, new challenges arise. The process doesn't have to be contentious but does have to be consistent, and grounded in facts, research, and the needs of the child.

While parent advocacy shouldn't set up an adversarial relationship between parents and educators, it often does. As the following sections detailing real-life experiences reveal, advocacy is not for the faint-hearted. It can get unpleasant, so be prepared.

Time is on Their Side. Not Yours.

Don't waste your time in interminable battles with those who just will not hear what you have to say. The stalling tactics employed by many who run and work in public schools can seriously affect your child's life chances.

A school system, like any bureaucracy, can drain your time and energy with meeting after meeting. Parents may be summoned to one meeting after another to discuss their child's difficulties in school, but rarely to address their specific dyslexic needs.

When the meetings don't go as planned, parents request more meetings with educators in the hopes of clearing up misunderstandings, setting a new, more positive path, and making plans for future success. This seems like a good, sensible strategy. But it rarely works.

School officials can string parents along for months and months, stretching into years, making endless vague suggestions, planning additional meetings and assessments, and suggesting the overused strategy of waiting to see what happens.

Direct questions are rarely answered, and can lead to endless, meaningless, and ultimately circular discussions, like this one:

Q: What is the reading approach you're using for my dyslexic child?

A: We use a variety of approaches to help your child.

Q: But is there one for dyslexia that you use for teaching reading?

A: We prefer to allow our teachers the opportunity to try out various methods.

Q: What kind of training does the teacher have to teach students with dyslexia?

A: All our teachers are credentialed to teach our students.

Q: Does the teacher have any specialized training in dyslexia?

A: The teacher is scheduled for professional development that our district is investing a lot of money in, which should take place in the spring or summer or fall, depending on the interest and enrollment.

Q: That's great but that's another school year; what will happen to my child's reading instruction until then?

A: We use a variety of approaches to help your child…

And so it goes.

Vague and misleading reassurances are given: "When your child decides to focus, he/she will learn to read." "Don't worry, it will come. You must be patient." "Give us six more weeks to try out another program."

If this sounds familiar, run for the hills, and take your child with you. The next steps for parents are: Find your child an in-person or online tutor who knows how to teach a student with dyslexia; learn how to tutor your child, or enroll your child in the nearest learning center or private school that provides students with dyslexia with the approach they need.

Otherwise you can spend years running down rabbit holes while educators and administrators do little to nothing to provide appropriate services but do keep you very busy with meeting after meeting that goes nowhere, and does nothing to improve your child's skills.

You Won't Believe Your Ears

While helping my son travel through the grades, negative comments were directed at me from a wide assortment of friends, family, teachers, administrators and community members.

The regular stuff included: "He'll grow out of it." "He just needs to focus, pay attention and work harder." "Don't worry, he's all boy." And "Didn't you ever read to him when he was little?"

From a family member: "We don't believe in dyslexia. We think you just need to be a little stricter with him and he'll learn to read."

From a friend: "Do you think it's really fair to other kids when he gets extra time to complete his assignments and they don't?"

From a high school teacher: "I know you have been a tenacious advocate for your son, but this is a very rigorous class, and he will be expected to perform."

From a Special Education case manager: "I don't want to work with your child anymore—you are just too demanding."

The comments were worse when I was advocating for other kids and their parents:

From an elementary school teacher: "I just don't have a magic wand that I can wave to teach him to read."

From a Special Ed administrator: "What parents want is a Cadillac when they're only entitled to a Chevy." In car-conscious California, a more contemporary analogy was recently used: "What parents want is a Tesla, when they're only entitled to a Prius."

From an elementary school principal: "Even though she enjoys art, we're going to take it away and give her two math classes instead."

From a principal during an IEP (speaking in a whisper about a single mom and her son): "This isn't a learning disability, it's a parenting problem."

From a high school science teacher in an IEP meeting: "This is the only student I've ever seen who has anxiety from his learning disability."

From a school psychologist during an IEP: "Oh, it's such a great idea to exit this child from Special Education. That way she escapes the stigma."

From a district superintendent: "I'm not convinced about this 1 in 5 number, and neither is our assistant superintendent in charge of elementary education."

The worst, most chilling comment of all came from a director of Special Education who couldn't understand my concern about a very troubled student: "We have a lot of dyslexic students who can't read, who have attempted suicide and have terrible home lives. What makes this one so special to you?"

I know a former case manager promoted to the position of Special Education Director at a high school. At a meeting to arrange remedial services for a dyslexic senior, who was reading at a first-grade level, I requested an Orton-Gillingham approach in reading. She leaned over to me and asked, "How do you spell that?"

After the meeting, she followed up: "What is that Orson-Guggenheim?" When I explained to her that it is the go-to, time-tested approach to reading for students with dyslexia, she brightened. "Oh, my son has dyslexia!"

"What kind of intervention is he receiving to help him with his reading?" I asked.

"Oh, he's not," she said. "But it's okay. They think it's something with his eyes, some kind of vision problem. He'll probably grow out of it."

This employee is paid well ($100,000+/yr) to know how to provide services for high school students in Special Education; more than 60 percent of the students on her caseload are qualified under Specific Learning Disability (mostly due to dyslexia). Her own son has dyslexia and, remarkably, she knows nothing at all about it.

Going Legal

Sometimes parents make a clear case and get appropriate services in return. Sometimes not. The educational bureaucracy is a well-funded, well-entrenched institution highly invested in maintaining control. It is resolutely inert and resistant to change.

When parents have exhausted all avenues—and *exhausted* is the perfect word—and believe their children are not receiving the Free Appropriate Public Education the law requires, they may have to take the fight to another level. If differences with the district continue, parents may decide to retain an attorney to file for a due process hearing or mediation, or even to litigate.

Any and all of this is time-consuming, costly in ways parents can't even imagine, and may not result in the outcome parents want—an appropriate education for their dyslexic child. It is very difficult for parents to go up against the virtually unlimited resources available to a school district, and even if you "win," it's doubtful that compensatory or remedial solutions are ever as good as timely and appropriate instruction would have been.

Burned Up and Burned Out

Don't convince yourself that you'll be the one who helps educators see the light, that if only they knew more about dyslexia, surely they would be eager to provide better services for your child and others, incorporating excellent teacher training and appropriate reading approaches.

How to address dyslexia in public schools is not a secret; it's simply been resisted for generations.

You can run yourself ragged thinking that you will change their minds, touch their hearts and make a substantial difference with just with one more meeting, one more reasoned discussion, one more persuasive e-mail. Before you know it, the school year is over, and you may not have made any progress—and you may have made people in the school system unhappy with you and your advocacy. As my son once said after realizing I'd had a particularly difficult day, "Mom, they don't want to hear what you have to say."

True enough. The burnout factor is real.

Much in the educational system keeps parent-advocates from banding together, since the approach to dyslexia is cloaked in confidentiality and treats each individual case as though it is completely unique from every other one. The education system has a way of making parents believe the issues presented by a dyslexic student are unusual and baffling—not common to 1 in 5 of the student population. Parents are kept from any way of contacting each other, creating on-campus support groups or realizing how many are separately dealing with the same issue. Keeping each family in its own separate silo with its own learning curve works for the bureaucrats but it is clearly not in the best interest of the child or the parents—nor does it help bring about much-needed change in the system.

This is where it gets tricky. By the time parents have fought the good fight for their own children, and developed the background knowledge and advocacy skills to do so, they are exhausted. Sick of dyslexia and all things related to the fighting the system. And when their kids are done, they are done. And they walk away. Taking their knowledge with them. Totally understandable.

While advocating for your child, do your best to avoid burnout by developing a support system to help with the work. Bounce around ideas and strategies, and share struggles and successes. Connections with others—in person and online—will help support your own emotional wellbeing in the often-tough battle to help your dyslexic child.

Keep motivated, stay strong, remain positive. Eventually the dysfunctional, bureaucratic, present-day approach to dyslexia in our educational system will be consigned to the dustbin of history—where it should have been dumped decades ago.

When Parents Have Dyslexia

Because of the genetic component of dyslexia, a significant number of parents advocating for their children have dyslexia themselves. They may feel guilt, anger, and sadness over passing it along. No parent with dyslexia wants their child to repeat the same struggles in school that they encountered,

It's not uncommon in a couple for the parent who doesn't have dyslexia to consciously or subconsciously blame the parent who does. A better way to look at it: The parent who has dyslexia has experience, insight and knowledge, as well as the recognition of the early signs that can be shared with the child, in a teamwork approach.

No one size fits all approach is right for every parent with dyslexia. Moms with dyslexia take quite different approaches in helping their children with dyslexia, as the following examples below illustrate:

Sarah, a dyslexic mother of two dyslexic sons was saddened when she realized that because of her dyslexia, she could not pass the Barton screener test in order to teach her boys the Barton Method, an effective approach for teaching reading. However, this accomplished and intelligent mom has also earned her Ph.D., and she holds a prestigious position at a major university. Let that be a reminder when you think about dyslexia and intelligence!

Gloria also has two sons, one dyslexic, one not. She provided early intervention and continued support for her dyslexic son through a private tutoring service. Now a straight-A student in high school, he's never been in Special Education, and is doing very well, with occasional extra tutoring, in his classes.

Erin, fed-up with the slowed-down pace and content of classes, lack of assistive technology and increased anxiety her son experienced in public school, opted to pull her dyslexic son out for homeschooling. She contracts with an experienced dyslexia tutor for web-based daily reading instruction, and with a speech therapist and an occupational therapist, paid for by her excellent insurance. She knows she is very lucky to have access to financial resources not available to everyone.

Along with having certain advantages in the advocacy realm, dyslexic parents face unique challenges. A return to the classroom to advocate for a child can be a trigger for previous negative experiences, a form of Post-Traumatic Stress Disorder. Studies have found high levels of anxiety among dyslexic parents, who can feel like they are back on the scene of their troubling childhood experiences once again. The classroom environment can trigger vivid reminders of bad school days, bad grades, bullying and worse. If you're a parent with dyslexia and need to attend a meeting on campus, consider bringing in a friend or another family member to offer support as you advocate.

Multicultural Dyslexia Awareness

With all its acronyms, specialized vocabulary and technical terms, the language used in DyslexiaLand is plenty difficult for native English speakers. Just imagine how difficult it might be for a non-English speaking parents to advocate for their children!

Nevertheless, against all odds, parents who are limited English speakers and who are extremely motivated, advocate for their children who may be English Language Learners themselves. Many of these students have worked very hard to learn English in school, but their parents may not have had the opportunity to do so. They likely cannot read to their children in English or help them with their homework.

Challenges with the language compound the struggle to get appropriate services; everything discussed must be interpreted and everything written must be translated—increasing the complexity of an already time-consuming process.

I've seen Spanish speakers handed a multi-page psychologist's report and an IEP written in English, and told that it would take eleven months to get it translated—just about in time for the next annual meeting!

More than language must be interpreted: Often it's a largely Anglo administration in charge of the complex bureaucracy that dispenses services to the minority/disadvantaged families requesting them. The entire subtext of a stressful meeting is one of inequality.

If, for example, parents don't know they have the right to ask for accommodations—or what accommodations they actually could ask for—and are limited in their English speaking ability, odds are the minority child with dyslexia will receive only limited assistance from school officials.

In 2013, Dr. Sally Shaywitz of the Yale Center for Creativity and Dyslexia hosted a symposium, *Dyslexia: A Civil Rights Issue for Our Time*, with Harry Belafonte as the keynote speaker. Out of that meeting came the "Multicultural Dyslexia Awareness Initiative," with the statement: "Education for all is the civil rights issue of today. We need to improve literacy levels in the multicultural community through increased education and awareness of dyslexia, the most common reading disability."

Student Self-Advocacy

We often hear educators tell students that they have to learn to self-advocate, but we rarely hear about anyone teaching the skills they need to do so. It's very important for students with dyslexia to understand the very basics: they have a uniquely wired brain that can make some tasks more difficult—especially academic tasks in reading, writing, spelling and math.

At the same time, they should know that dyslexia also means they have some real strengths in creatively thinking outside the box, seeing patterns that others might not recognize, and working collaboratively with others. When students understand their learning style, and what they need in the way of accommodations to succeed, it helps them feel more confident and in control of their own education.

For younger children, knowing the basics is empowering. To help them connect with a teacher, parents can provide a fact sheet, or even a laminated card they can keep in their backpack that explains their needs, their accommodations and any other appropriate information.

This is particularly helpful when they encounter a new teacher, substitute teacher, or at the beginning of the new school year.

Older students need to be empowered to express their needs to guarantee that they receive appropriate accommodations in the classroom. A little role-playing at home can help them gain confidence in their ability to communicate effectively with educators, and obtain what they need in school.

Family Matters and Teamwork

One concerned adult-turned-advocate can turn a child's life around. More often than not this champion is a parent, though let's give a shout-out for the many grandparents, aunts, uncles, family friends, and others who step up to advocate for a child.

In most cases, mom takes the lead in dyslexia advocacy, but moms are obviously not the only ones involved. Advocacy is a team effort, and best accomplished when every member has a role to play, whether it's mom, dad, partner, trusted friend, neighbor, relative or even a professional advocate.

Not every family has a dad, and this subject may not be politically correct to address, but it can be of huge benefit when dad is involved in his child's education, particularly in advocating for services.

Just as it may be unfair—even infuriating—to hardworking moms, when dads are singled out and appreciated for "babysitting" their children, be warned that much to women's consternation, dads are often the recipients of much praise for taking the time out of *their* busy schedules to meet with teachers and administrators to discuss the education of their children.

Like it or not, unfair as it might be, when dad, or another father figure, shows up—whether dad is a gardener, an insurance broker or an engineer—the male energy in the room changes the dynamic, and often alters the outcome in positive ways. Men tend to be results-oriented, may add a sense of authority and urgency, and their presence tends to heighten focus on the matter at hand: getting appropriate services for the student.

When dad speaks up, educators listen. Dads may quickly grow impatient at the lack of progress their children are making, and the lack of effective approaches the educators are offering—and express their frustration more directly than most moms might consider appropriate. More than once I've heard a father cut through all the talk and say to educators in exasperation, "All we're asking is for you people to do your job!"

That kind of comment, delivered with such an obvious determination to fix the situation, tends to get results. When my husband and I committed to a series of meetings to get private reading instruction for our son paid for by the school district, we decided to play "good cop/bad cop."

My role was to patiently make the informed and reasoned case, discuss the test results, and the multiple concerns about our son's academic struggles. His was to emphasize the need for appropriate, professional educational services delivered on time and with excellent, measurable results.

Every time educators would give an excuse why they couldn't possibly comply—even though they admitted they could not offer any appropriate reading instruction for a student with dyslexia, and asserted that wait-and-see was an effective strategy—my unflinching husband would return to his mantra, "Nevertheless, we want Lindamood-Bell, and we have no more time to waste." Eventually, the district officials ran out of arguments, realized that we, as a team, would not be put off with platitudes or patchwork programs, and agreed to our request.

Each member of the team advocating for a student needs to be on the same page before and during any meeting with educators. Nothing is more self-defeating than a couple or other team members arguing over policies, strategies, or approaches in front of educators. Whatever the state of the relationship, make sure it is a unified front before and during the meeting.

In some families, one parent (uh, usually dad) may think that all this time spent on advocacy is just babying the student, and that what's really needed is more discipline, fewer privileges, and a sink-or-swim approach. If that is the case in your home or family, know that such an attitude will not help the child with dyslexia.

Dyslexia Warrior Moms

There is nothing like the persistence and determination of a mother (or a father, but by and large, this is a mother-driven movement) on a mission—and mothers of children with dyslexia have proven their ability as disruptors and innovators who question the status quo. They are true agents of change.

This legion of determined mothers will not be ignored the way generations before them were. Call them "Dyslexia Warrior Moms," "Dyslexia Mama Bears," or "The Dyslexia Sisterhood." Whatever the brand, the mission is the same: stand up, speak out and help dyslexic children achieve their full potential no matter what.

Moms have mastered media to form a powerful social network for support and the sharing of resources. The moms may not see each other often, know one another in any other context except dyslexia circles, and may have wildly dissimilar political beliefs, but when they do meet, it's a warm and deep connection. They speak the same language, share the same frustrations, and celebrate the same successes. There is strength in numbers, and in a unified message: The educational needs of children with dyslexia must be properly addressed and mothers will not go away. Dyslexia Warrior Moms will work in every way possible to get their message out until real institutional change occurs.

Dyslexia Warrior Moms are the embodiment of the Margaret Mead quote: "Never doubt that a small group of thoughtful, committed citizens can change the world; indeed, it's the only thing that ever has."

How to Address the School Board

Parents may want to make a statement to the school board to affect positive change in dyslexia at the local level. A few insights will help you be more effective in making your presentation. Remember that whenever you speak or write, you are building a relationship with decision-makers.

1) Think about to whom you are speaking: School board trustees are dedicated professional community members who volunteer their time to provide oversight of the administration and business conducted by the school district. These elected officials work as a leadership team to help guide the policies and procedures to serve the community.

2) Remember that your comments are recorded for broadcast on public television as well as archived on the district's website.

3) Your comments are time-limited so plan and practice them within the time allowed.

4) Fill out a speaker slip well before the meeting begins; be sure to fill it out legibly to make it easier to

pronounce your name correctly when it's your turn to speak.

5) Check the agenda; you may intend to speak at public comment about an issue not on that meeting's agenda, or you may want to speak to an issue that is on agenda—if so, be sure to indicate that on your speaker slip. Pay attention to the agenda, and be ready to speak when you're called on. Remember that time estimates are just that, and sometimes agendas are juggled to accommodate a large number of attendees for a single item.

6) Be respectful in your tone, and appreciative of the opportunity to speak out; state your name, your profession and why you are speaking on the issue. Remember that a little passion goes a long way, and a memorable personal anecdote about dyslexia that illustrates a larger truth can be very effective.

7) As you craft your comments in advance, think about the wider audience that will hear them. Remember that word travels fast and is long remembered; you don't want to leave people squirming in their seats or wishing you would just stop speaking. Even if you are upset, you may want to reconsider any notion of "blasting" a teacher, an administrator or a policy. Anything you have to communicate can be done in a thoughtful and a respectful way.

8) You may also express your concerns or issues in writing with an email to school board trustees,

knowing that it will likely be circulated to other members as well as to the Superintendent and others. Bring a copy of your comments, and make them available to members of the press, if requested.

9) It's respectful to thank the trustees, and when you are finished with your comments, to return to your seat and remain in the audience at least until discussion of the agenda item or public comment is complete.

10) If you want to respond to or speak to others, wait until after you leave the hearing room. You may want to consider writing a follow-up note or sending a copy of your comments after the hearing, if you feel like that's appropriate.

Parents' Advocacy Plan

1) **Learn about learning differences and how they affect a child's pathway in school.** Learn about dyslexia, dysgraphia, dyscalculia, and/or others like auditory processing disorder and visual processing disorder. Recognize that this is nuanced and it is important to address each issue differently and appropriately.

2) **Learn how to work** with classroom teachers, educators and administrators to remove the obstacles and focus on opportunities by creating a pathway that maximizes the child's potential. Research your school district's history, corporate culture, and

how it addresses dyslexia and Special Education. Develop relationships and try to find an ally—at least one educator in the system who you think you can trust to help you get what your child needs.

3) **Learn about successful strategies.** Read up on Orton-Gillingham and Structured Word Inquiry, learn about assistive technology and understand appropriate accommodations that fit your child's learning style.

4) **Learn all you can about** reading programs, successful interventions, and professional development in your school district. Insist that your child be taught reading with the Orton-Gillingham approach. Realize that many school districts lack programs or appropriately trained teachers, and may try to substitute computer programs for vastly more effective one-on-one teaching.

5) **Find a way:** If the school doesn't provide services, you'll need to pay for a tutor or remedial reading services for your child. Make certain this professional is trained and skilled in successfully addressing dyslexia. Alternatively, parents might decide to learn appropriate methodology (i.e. the Barton System) and, with the help of online resources, teach their children.

6) **Find a support group** (or start one if necessary); network and educate yourself as much as possible about how to be a successful advocate; attend

workshops, lectures and seminars. Learn about nonprofits that are dedicated to serving the community of learning differences and seek out their information, resources and advocacy services. Read about (and consider joining) local, national and even international organizations dedicated to supporting the research, education and political lobbying efforts of the dyslexia community. Become a part of the Decoding Dyslexia movement in your state and/or local area.

7) **Learn about Special Education, if you decide to go that route.** This is a huge undertaking. You will have to understand Parental Rights and how to use them; the difference between an IEP and a 504 Plan; how to help set goals, understand assessments, accommodations and timelines, and work cooperatively to determine the best approach for your child as required by state and federal law.

8) **Write it down.** Always send a follow up email or note to offer your thanks, and to provide a written record for the conversation or meeting that you had with a teacher or school officials.

TUTORS

FRIENDS

TEACHERS

PARENTS

10

Dyslexia At Home and in the Community

L et's remember how much time children spend *out-side* of school!

Combine a loving home, parental awareness, support of strengths and appropriate accommodations, and your child with dyslexia can thrive. Extended family and friends can be a big help, too.

While that proverb, "It takes a village to raise a child" may be true, significant help from the "village" for your child with dyslexia can be hard to come by. Nevertheless, thanks to much good work accomplished in the schools by students, parents and advocates—along with lots of networking online and off—the word is getting out and communities small and large are becoming more dyslexia-friendly.

"Dyslexia-Friendly Community" is not yet a phrase in popular use, but increasingly government and businesses are at least hearing the good word, and policies that accommodate people with dyslexia may be commonplace one day. Meanwhile, parents can help their child navigate that vast world beyond the school fence with proven strategies that make life easier.

Effects on Family Life

That phrase, "You're only as happy as your least happy child," certainly applies in DyslexiaLand. Dealing with dyslexia can really put stress on the family dynamic.

Figuring out how to help your child through school is time-consuming, and it can all-too-easily shift the focus onto one member of the family at the expense of the others. Keep your multiple commitments in balance and maintain your perspective.

In two-parent households, it's common for one parent—usually mom—to be the primary advocate. It's not uncommon for the other parent—who may not understand the issues associated with dyslexia in the same kind of detail as the advocate does—to become angry, raise concerns that the child is "being coddled," that the parent/advocate is "overprotective," or that all the child needs to do is work harder and focus more.

This difficulty in accepting the reality of dyslexia can cause significant discord in the home and negatively affect the child's learning issues. While not necessarily easy, it's optimal if parents—and the rest of the family—are on the same page when it comes to dealing with learning differences.

Keep your perspective: children with dyslexia have much more to offer than all those school struggles would indicate; be mindful of those many special gifts and don't lose sight of them. Never begrudge children the amount of time or effort you spend helping them get a good education. Regard this as a gift from one generation to another, one of the most valuable gifts you could ever give.

Siblings—as well as the child with dyslexia—should be taught to understand the issue with compassion and grace. As with so many family issues, learning to strike the right balance takes give-and-take and trial and error before figuring it out. Be patient and understanding with everyone.

Lighten up, keep your sense of humor. The way kids with dyslexia see the world is altogether special—in a good and sometimes quite amusing way! Celebrate those fun moments when your child delights in "flutter byes" (butterflies), "alligator juice" (Gatorade) and leaves a note for you, signed "Your Sun."

Friends and Extended Family

While well-meaning friends and family may want to help you and your child with dyslexia, be aware that they may need some schooling in the best ways to show their concern and support. Proactively inform them of your child's learning style and—depending on the closeness of the relationship and their level of sensitivity—your child's strengths and struggles. They may have experiences to share or even insights about other family members with dyslexia.

While many famous and accomplished individuals with dyslexia are willing to share their stories, many adults "in real life" who have dyslexia are uncomfortable doing so. Don't automatically assume friends, relatives or members of your community who have dyslexia will want to talk about it with your child.

Gift-giving alert: Regardless of the good intention of the giver, gifts such as books guaranteed to build brain power, flash cards, spelling games, educational software and so on will likely not be well-received by a child who struggles in school. Instead, these items reinforce low self-esteem and can become additional sources of embarrassment and frustration. Before a gift-giving occasion arises, parents might suggest an item that reinforces a child's strengths and interests instead, such as art supplies, sports equipment, a puzzle, or tickets to a performance.

Communicate about dyslexia simply and without an emotional charge, by informing others about your child's strengths and interests outside of school. Say something like: "Yes, Katya has dyslexia. It's a neurologically based learning difference and we're learning how to deal with it. What more would you like to know? And by the way, she really enjoys playing tennis lately."

Virtually all kids, particularly those who struggle in school, really like it when well-meaning adults make an inquiry other than, "So how are you doing in school?" Fill them in about other interests and activities that are part of your child's life. "Riley has been researching and building a catapult in the afternoons. Would you like to know more about that?"

If you should have the unfortunate experience of speaking with someone who asserts, "Well, I just don't believe in dyslexia"—or worse—do your best to inform and enlighten with kindness and understanding. "Well, Alex is certainly an example of the reality of dyslexia, just like 1 in 5 other children. Let me tell you what it's like."

Or just move on, agree to disagree, and go where the love is.

Homework

It's called Home Work—work that a student is expected to address and complete at home. Your home. His or her home. It may be an extension of schoolwork, but it is often the single most stressful part of parenting a school-age child. A parent is expected to be the enforcer, the taskmaster who guarantees that homework gets done.

Consider the plight of the student with dyslexia who barely manages to get through one stress-filled day after another, faced with hours upon hours of additional work to complete before getting some sleep and starting all over the next day.

Many homework assignments involve rote learning: memorization of spelling words; the multiplication
tables; state or world capitals; the completion of a few
dozen math problems or filling out worksheets. This kind
of busy work does little to enhance learning—particularly for a big-picture thinker with dyslexia—and typically
succeeds only in frustrating child and parents alike.

Similarly, there's no better way to rob a child of the
pleasures of a good story than to turn a book into a
nightly assignment with a set of questions to answer.
Take an adventurous 16-year-old boy, excited to have
the chance to read *Into the Wild* for English class. But
the teacher's nightly worksheets required tedious attention to the tiniest details in the book, and took all the
sense of big adventure out of the story of a young man's
desperate search for meaning in the Alaskan wilderness.

What's a parent to do when the homework is overwhelming, your child is crying, and you are stressed out
trying to get it done?

Exercise your parental rights and write a note to the
teacher that indicates your child got so far, and is done.
A good rule of thumb is 10 minutes of homework per
grade level: for example no more than 30 minutes in
third grade, 60 minutes in sixth grade, and so on.

Homework should not be allowed to become a
source of anxiety, family tension, or misery at home.
If and when that happens, it's time to work with the
teacher, or other school official to make adjustments

to the kinds and volume of homework. (The type and amount of homework should be included in a student's IEP or 504 plan.) Life's too short to have homework turn home life upside-down!

Details, Details, Details

Lack of organizational skills, time management problems, and clutter everywhere can make family life difficult with a child with dyslexia. Think of these challenges as opportunities to teach life skills in positive ways. Instead of using words, try labeling drawers, closets and organizers with pictures, photos or color codes. Use a digital clock rather than an analog one. Reduce clutter and confusion over toy choices by keeping only what is essential.

Purchase clothing that is multi-purpose and well-coordinated so that everything goes with everything else (and you may have to remove stiff labels and avoid scratchy fabrics if your child is particularly sensitive to them). Deal proactively with the issue of shoe-tying by purchasing shoes with Velcro closures, or new elastic alternatives to laces.

Choose your battles. Anticipate issues, and give up expectations of perfection.

Extracurricular Activities

Your child with dyslexia may struggle to read, but may love to play music, act, dance, or play soccer. Your child may also enjoy filmmaking, fiber arts, martial arts,

Scouting, or writing computer code. These group activities and individual pursuits should be encouraged and supported as much as possible.

While providing many rewards, extracurricular activities also present challenges to the child with dyslexia. Kids may have difficulty remembering complicated training exercises, reading music, or fulfilling the expectations of coaches or other instructors. Be proactive with adult leaders: An open, honest discussion about your child's strengths and weaknesses, as well as suggestions about how to accommodate them will help avoid misunderstandings and improve relationships and outcomes all around.

Tips for Playtime

* **Right and Left Awareness** Help your child, even if it requires inking an R and an L on a pair of shoes, or making an L with the left forefinger and thumb.

* **Anticipate Confusion** When coaches get overly ambitious devising complicated or confusing workouts that require processing a sequence of maneuvers; you might need to intervene and explain your child's learning style, and offer tips for success. (The older your athlete gets and the higher the level of competition, the trickier it gets to diplomatically make suggestions to a coach on behalf of your child.) Some coaches, though, like to simplify things, and welcome an idea to enhance performance. An

oft-repeated phrase by Craig Moropoulos, longtime winning coach of the Santa Barbara City College football team, is, "Don't try to do too much."

* **Musical Notes** When music instruction requires reading the notes, your child's enthusiasm may wane. Seek strategies that work, including playing by ear if necessary.

* **Memorization Techniques** When learning lines for a play, many children with dyslexia have an uncanny ability to memorize all the parts instead of relying on the script. At the very least, highlight your student's part throughout the script, and develop cues that work.

What's on the Menu?

You may notice that your dyslexic child always orders the same thing at a restaurant. The cause may not be non-adventurous tastes, but rather due to difficulty reading the book-like menu. Some children may compensate for their difficulties reading it by pointing to a picture, or by figuring out a corresponding number—like #7 the Combo Platter.

A casual dining establishment can also pose some issues: These restaurants often feature extensive menus posted above the cash register where you order as the line follows behind you. This can be daunting because it's easy to feel rushed and overwhelmed—for anyone unfamiliar with the offerings—while trying to decipher the descriptions.

So it can be a safe and face-saving strategy to just order a turkey sandwich, a vegetarian burrito or a cheeseburger when it's a good bet it's on the menu—and there won't be any embarrassment.

Parents can anticipate this issue and gently note some of the other offerings available, describing dishes your child might like, making a suggestion for something different, or by describing your own choice. But then again, some kids might just want to stick with their comfort level and what they know.

Dyslexia as a Public Health Issue

The consequences of low literacy rates are devastating to every single individual, as well as the community as a whole. When the local school district fails to deliver reading instruction that is explicit, structured, and multi-sensory—that is to say, teach students in the way they learn—it becomes an issue of public health.

According to *The Washington Post*, the effects include: "Limited ability to obtain and understand essential information; unemployment: the unemployment rate is 2–4 times higher among those with little schooling than among those with Bachelor's degrees; lower income; lower-quality jobs; reduced access to life-long learning and professional development; precarious financial position; little value is given to education and reading within the family, and this often leads to inter-generational transmission of illiteracy; lower self-esteem, which can lead to isolation; impact on health: illiterate individuals have more workplace accidents, take longer to recover and more often misuse medication through ignorance of health care resources and because they have trouble reading and understanding the relevant information (warnings, dosage, contraindications, etc.)."

Dyslexia is a high-stakes issue that doesn't go away by ignoring it. Creating Dyslexia-Friendly Communities where all are respected, taught appropriately, and provided an opportunity to succeed makes all the difference.

Dyslexia in the Religious Community

It bears repeating that reading out loud is one of the most searing experiences for anyone with dyslexia. Parents may take steps to make sure their children are not called on in school, but forget about the possibility that they may be asked to read out loud—and have to study and write—as part of their religious education as well.

Consider the example of James Middleton, brother of Catherine who married Prince William of England in 2011. During the royal wedding, James, who has severe dyslexia, read a Bible passage from Romans to an estimated audience of two billion people. He later revealed that he had carefully written the passage out phonetically, and his flawless delivery was one of the highlights of the ceremony. (You can watch it on You-Tube.)

My son loved the multi-sensory church services of our faith: smelling the incense, looking at the icons, listening to the chanting and music—all with no reading required. But he balked at going to Sunday school. Lessons prepared by Sunday school teachers required some of the same kind of reading and writing expected of him at Monday through Friday school.

For kids with dyslexia, religious education is a bit too much like, well, school. The are often asked to color Bible scenes within the lines, copy Scripture from the board, memorize passages, read aloud, and neatly complete worksheets.

Let's not forget that the three dominant monotheistic religions predate widespread literacy. For thousands of years Judaism, Christianity, and Islam shared faith and traditions with stories and art.

Religious leaders are starting to realize that significant numbers of their flock are getting left behind by taking an overly school-like approach to sharing the faith. "Demystifying Dyslexia," an article in a special edition of *Christian Educator Magazine* asks pastors and lay educators to teach kids with dyslexia in the way they learn:

Find ways to celebrate the creative genius of your dyslexic students and allow them to use their talents for God's kingdom. When the children's ministry team intentionally showcases the strengths and talents of these students, their God-confidence will soar, and church will be an exciting place with unlimited opportunity to explore worship.

As kids get older, the requirements for participation in organized religious activities get more demanding: studying Hebrew for Bar Mitzvah and Bat Mitzvahs; reading in Latin in the Catholic Church or in Greek or Russian in the Orthodox Church; remembering Bible verses; reading Scripture, perhaps with the expectation of reading aloud from the pulpit.

Beware of religious extremists who disdain the very concept of learning differences, and what they term the "the myth of dyslexia," or who believe that dyslexia is simply an excuse for laziness or a liberal excuse for poor teaching practices. Ignore them. They know not what they do or say—or who they hurt in the process.

Divine Intervention

✸ Communicate with those in your faith-based community who are in a position to assist your child. Share and come up with ways to help.

* Modify lessons or make other arrangements to make the material more accessible.

* Determine ways your child can participate in the religious life of your congregation other than with the written word, or devise workarounds when necessary.

* Check out the schedule at faith-based camps before signing your child up for a week. You may need to alert camp directors and counselors if there are readings and study sessions. Remember that much like Sunday School, "Vacation Bible School" type programs can be reading-intensive, and not at all a fun vacation for a child with dyslexia.

At Home with Dyslexia

1) **Think back to your own academic history,** and also ask if other family members had reading struggles. You might be surprised to learn that real estate wheeler-dealer Uncle Bill wasn't much for reading and could not spell at all. Parents often recognize their *own* dyslexia while in the process of figuring out what's happening with their own struggling child.

2) **Identify** how dyslexia affects your child, both academically and emotionally. Be vigilant about keeping the child's emotional well-being intact.

3) **Understand** that your child's needs will change over time and know how to continue to receive proper services through elementary, junior high, high

school and beyond by anticipating and implementing appropriate transitions.

4) **Maintain family life** and balance the needs of everyone, not just the child with dyslexia.

5) **Support your child's interests and strengths.** Many children with dyslexia have talent in music, drama, art, sports or science. Resist the urge to cut out those activities in order to focus on traditional academics. Your child needs these creative outlets, and your understanding of how they add meaning.

6) **Provide role models** and educate your child about his or her learning style, strengths and where support might be needed. Look for age-appropriate books and videos for children with dyslexia.

7) **Remember that reading and spelling skill do not equal intelligence**. Make certain your child is not defined by their ability to read or spell. Early struggles must not be allowed to define a child's emotional well-being or sense of confidence.

8) **Develop advocacy skills** and teach your child how to self-advocate, Help your child understand what dyslexia is all about, and how to own it.

11

What You Need to Know Before You Go

Y ou will be better prepared for "Traveling through the Grades" (Part III in *DyslexiaLand*) if you understand the potential financial implications to your family and review what I call "The Ten Essentials." Review these field-tested practicalities and make use of them in your travels. And for a bit of a spiritual boost, find comfort from a modified version of the "Serenity Prayer."

Costs Associated with Dyslexia

The cost of living and learning in DyslexiaLand is high.

Often surprisingly high.

Public schools provide less funding these days for non-academic activities, and most parents accept that they will likely need to help fund their children's extra-curricular activities: sports instruction and team travel, band, cheerleading, choral, dance, drama, ski club, robotics, and the list goes on.

And parents know and accept they may need to step up financially to pay for tutoring for their child, when it's not provided onsite at the school, to "catch up" on academic core subjects in the lower grades. And they acknowledge the need to get extra help for challenging classes in middle school and high school in classes like advanced math or science, advanced placement English and preparation for the ACT or SAT.

But parents do *not* expect to have to pay for private instruction in order for their children to learn to read, write, spell, and do math. However, parents of children with dyslexia are often compelled to pay for such instruction when schools fail at their most essential responsibility. And it tends to frustrate them. It is completely unfair that parents of students with dyslexia have to bear this financial burden when public schools fail at this most basic mission.

Maddening and frustrating? Absolutely. And often very costly, too. The highly specific instruction needed to teach children with dyslexia in the way they learn is not cheap. Depending on the amount of remediation needed, such instruction can be a significant investment of time and money. Once a child falls behind and needs remediation, it can take from six months to three years (or more) of intervention to "catch up."

For a child with dyslexia to receive appropriate professional services, you will need to hire a qualified individual with significant training and experience in direct, multi-sensory, structured language instruction (that is to say, with an Orton-Gillingham approach). Carefully select that tutor, so that you don't waste your time or money. Just about anyone can claim to be a tutor, an academic coach or an educational consultant, since no commonly accepted standards exist or credentials are required for a tutor to prove competence in teaching a student with dyslexia.

Educational therapists and those who have completed an extensive Orton-Gillingham training are experts who command top dollar—that is, typically upward from $50 per hour, depending on where you live.

Other parents may choose to send their child with dyslexia to a private school designed specifically to meet their needs. These schools provide the small-group setting, project-based learning and the appropriate reading instruction for dyslexic students, but they are extremely expensive—some costing as much for a year of Kindergarten as a year of tuition in a private college. This private option is not available in many areas of the country.

Parents can go the legal route to compel their school district to pay for Orton-Gillingham instruction, but it's no easy task. First they must establish that no program exists within the district to teach children with dyslexia in the way they learn; next they must convince administrators that the approach offered by the private individual or non-public agency is consistent with the federally guaranteed "Free Appropriate Public Education." It may happen as part of a closed-door settlement between the district, the parents and the education provider. Or it may require the parents to file for due process, or even a lawsuit. In such cases, parents will need to retain the services of an expert advocate or attorney experienced in such matters. All of this comes at great personal and financial cost.

School districts may have an open contract with a well-known service provider such as Lindamood-Bell, or they may maintain a list of approved private individuals or other non-public agencies that provide the educational services they do not.

When agreeing to contract for private educational services for a student, a school district will often require parents to sign a settlement agreement, complete with a nondisclosure clause. The amount of money school districts agree to pay varies widely from a few thousand dollars for instruction or summer tutoring services to placement in a private dyslexia boarding school, located halfway across the country.

Parents—who do not have dyslexia—may choose to learn how to teach their own children with dyslexia, particularly with the well-regarded Barton System. The Barton System is split into ten levels, which means the parent/tutor doesn't need to learn—or pay for—the entire system before starting. Based on Orton-Gillingham, the Barton System is designed for 1-to-1 tutoring. (Parents can hire a tutor trained in that system if they prefer that to teaching their child.)

What You Need to Know

If you think you can get away cheap by popping into one of those franchised learning centers for a few hours of instruction or by buying educational games, think again. Parents should not waste money on the popularly advertised computer approaches and programs that are not designed for children with dyslexia: Hooked on Phonics or The Phonics Game, Reading Recovery, Accelerated Reader, Brain Gym. Avoid most commercial learning center chains, that claim to have (non-Orton-Gillingham) programs that work for students with dyslexia or that claim to help children with dyslexia by providing nutritional information and giving them exercises such as walking over a balance beam. Be very wary of those that make big promises or that offer their own financing, or require you to sign up for many sessions in advance.

In addition to the basic Orton-Gillingham private reading instruction, parents may also decide to provide private assessments, private support in speech and/ or occupational therapy, and private consultation in assistive technology. These extra services can add up to many thousands of dollars per year. You may be doubly hit financially, with the need to support your dyslexic child's strengths — with lessons in art, music, sports or other possibly pricey endeavors.

Yet, if it is what your child needs to survive in school, it may just be that you have to do whatever you must to pay for it. In order to pay for both tutoring and high-level youth baseball expenses, my husband and I made the financial choices to drive 10- to 15-year-old cars, cut way back on eating in restaurants, put off vacations, and delayed home upgrades and all but the most critical home repairs.

In order to pay for these expenses, parents have been known to take a second mortgage on their homes, borrow money from their own parents, re-allocate college funds, tap into retirement plans, and take a second (or third) job.

As painful as it might be, most parents regard the cost of private instruction for their children with dyslexia as money well spent, since leaving instruction up to the schools will not likely result in a positive outcome. Invest your time and resources wisely, and take care of your dyslexic child.

Eight Great Ways to Get Help

When stymied by public schools, parents of dyslexic children often learn to be very resourceful in order to obtain assessments and appropriate reading instruction in the community. We must acknowledge that because these services require substantial amount of time, the associated costs may be prohibitive. Still there are options that parents can research and pursue. They include:

1) **Scottish Rite** The fraternal and charitable organization operates nearly 200 speech and language intervention clinics free of charge in the United States

and Canada. Services vary depending on location, and waiting lists can be long, but worth it. Reading instruction typically used is an Orton-Gillingham approach known as Take Flight. The organization even operates the Luke Waites Center for Dyslexia & Learning Disorders, at Scottish Rite Hospital in Dallas. Established in 1965, it was named after Dr. Lucius Waites, a pioneer in addressing dyslexia. The full-service center offers dyslexia assessments, outreach, research and training for educators.

2) **Services at hospitals and medical centers** As noted above, the medical establishment has stepped in to provide dyslexia diagnostic and reading remediation services in many locations across the country. Do your research to find the one that meets your needs closest to home.

3) **Services at universities** Many universities also offer assessment and tutoring services, often in conjunction with their schools of education. Their assessments and other services may be conducted by graduate students earning their hours required for earning their credentials or degrees, but they typically are closely supervised by senior academic staff members. There may be long waiting lists, but the price is often substantially below market rate.

4) **Non-profit organizations** There may be a dyslexia reading center in your area that offers sliding scale for its services.

5) **Barter or trade** I know many educational therapists and Orton-Gillingham trained educators who
have come up with innovative ways to help families
obtain reading instruction in exchange for specialized services they can offer without the exchange of
currency. It may be worth a discussion!

6) **Hybrid online charter/homeschool opportunities**
In some places, there are online public charter
schools that actually pay parents a modest amount
to obtain services. In my Southern California location,
an organization known as Inspire Charter Schools
offers a stipend of $2800, and a list of approved
vendors, including qualified reading instructors.

7) **Public schools designed for dyslexic students**
With each passing year, more educators realize they
can successfully dedicate an entire school campus
to serve the needs of dyslexic students. Tuition-free
public dyslexia schools include: GRASP Academy
in Jacksonville, FL; KEY Academy in Baton Rouge,
LA; MAX Charter School in Thibodaux, LA; Lakes &
Bridges Charter School in Easley, SC; Academy for
Literacy, Learning & Innovation Excellence in Colorado Springs, CO.

8) **Boon Philanthropy** Teachers who want to obtain
training in explicit multi-sensory literacy instruction
and Early Literacy Programs can apply for scholar-
ships with this non-profit dedicated to addressing

what they term the "crisis in reading instruction in the U.S."

The Ten Essentials

Your trip through DyslexiaLand requires a little tech savvy, and the adoption of a certain attitude toward the journey, the destination, and the people you meet along the way.

1) **On your way online** The amount of dyslexia resources is simply astonishing: websites, podcasts, Pinterest pages, webinars, and lots and lots of YouTube videos.

2) **Research skills** Realize that you are going to need to educate yourself in the particulars of your child's needs. Become a parent on a mission to find out everything you need to know to help.

3) **A positive attitude** Do everything you can to stay upbeat and on top of the situation. Your child will be fine as long as you're involved, informed and intent on getting the help needed at every point along the way. Don't let the bureaucrats get you down!

4) **Facebook and more** A Facebook page is devoted to just about every aspect of dyslexia, from support across the country (and around the world) to your own hometown. Connecting on social media brings levels of expertise and an information network not possible at any other time, or in any other medium. Bonus: you'll develop a strong network of friends,

who you may get to know in ways other than with your mutual involvement in dyslexia.

5) **Understand how bureaucracies function** You've dealt with the IRS, the healthcare system, the Department of Motor Vehicles and the cable company, so you have a pretty good idea about the way they work. The school district is not much different: It is a monopoly, a set of rigid practices, polices and procedures, and a large, taxpayer-funded workforce dedicated to protecting the status quo. You—and your child's needs with dyslexia—are seen as an impediment to the smooth functioning of the well-oiled machine. Keep this in mind in your interactions with educators and administrators. School districts have lofty mottoes like, "Every Child, Every Chance, Every Day," or "Building A Better World One Student At A Time" or "Preparing Students For Success In A Changing World," but it's questionable how their mottoes are actually put into practice.

6) **A fiercely protective spirit** Your priority at all times is to protect your child from hurtful practices while securing the best possible education. Do not confuse these two priorities, or you'll end up regretting the lapse. It may take more courage than you ever realized you have, but summoning up the Mama Bear or Papa Bear protective instinct when your little one is in trouble is pretty easy to access.

7) **Share your knowledge, carefully** You will likely realize early in your journey that you have learned more about dyslexia than most educators or administrators you encounter. Be thoughtful and collaborative in how you present your information, understanding that you're treading on their turf, and know that most of them will not be pleased to hear from a parent whose expertise outshines their own. You may be inclined to think that they would welcome the information; more likely it will evoke a response that is defensive, angry, or suspicious.

8) **Deliberate action** Manage your time. You don't have to sign anything if you're not ready. You don't have to answer an email, or take a phone call in the moment if you're not prepared to address the issue at hand. You can even postpone a meeting to accommodate your schedule, to arrange for a support person or advocate to accompany you to an IEP.

9) **Try not to take things personally** On occasion, questions will be posed that will take you aback: "What's the matter at home?" "Don't you ever read to her?" "Don't you think you're babying him with these accommodations?" Be forgiving and willing to consider the source: They may not realize what they're saying.

10) **Determination to succeed** While it is a long jour-ney, with daunting tasks to perform along the way, your persistence and determination will win out

every time. The trip may not look like you expect it to right now—there may be diversions and different pathways, so keep flexible, consider your options, and remain committed to your goal: To provide your child with a pathway to success and the opportunity to reach her/his full potential.

The Serenity Prayer

The Serenity Prayer by theologian Reinhold Niebuhr offers parents of children with dyslexia comfort and wise counsel:

God, grant me the serenity to accept the things I cannot change,
Courage to change the things I can,
And wisdom to know the difference.

Serenity. Courage. Wisdom. In equal amounts, they can help guide your way and give you comfort on your journey through DyslexiaLand. When your child struggles to read year after year and you must navigate a system that's as uncaring as it is unbending, a parent's level of frustration can rise to an almost unbearable degree.

While remaining serene, you may have to summon the "Courage to change the things I *cannot accept.*" No parent can accept a school system that cannot or will not properly educate their dyslexic child.

In such times, parents must remain focused, not as the school culture might have it on the mundane and soul-sapping goals of assignment-by-assignment, day-to-day, grade-by-grade, but rather, in the big-picture view of what it all adds up to, how it affects your child, yourself and your family. And, importantly, how the short-term affects your child in the long term.

Miss Evelyn, my daughter's fourth-grade teacher at the Waldorf school once told me, "I'm not teaching my students for this year, I'm teaching them for the people they will become when they are in their thirties."

At the time she said that, I realized her comment was important, but that was long before I ever learned anything about dyslexia. Her words have come back to me many times and helped me remember that there's a timetable to deal with that is far more important than the minute-to-minute examination that scrutinizes and quantifies and assigns a grade to virtually every move, every page, every word.

The greater goal for parents is developing a solid foundation for fulfilled, happy, and self-actualized children to reach their full potential and achieve their dreams.

PART III

TRAVELING THROUGH THE GRADES

Shouting and laughing in the late afternoon waves, two 11-year-old boys have a blast, riding their boogie boards as dolphins literally jump out of the sparkling water a few yards away from them. They ride bikes, fish off the pier, camp out in the backyard. One plays guitar, the other plays baseball.

Life is good in the summertime, with memorable moments and long afternoons filled with endless activity; a time when all that matters is playing sports, hanging out with friends, and learning by discovery.

It's a world apart from the confines of the classroom, especially for the boy with dyslexia, where every day of the school year is a struggle with words on the page, and every night is a battle to get the homework done.

Outside of school, these joyful, active boys relate to each other as total equals, each with his own particular skills, likes and dislikes. But in the same class, at the same school, one is considered smart and one is considered dumb, lazy and unmotivated to learn. And those labels are based on how they read, write and spell, and everybody knows who can read and who can't.

Reading words—trying to figure out what they mean, and how they sound—and writing words—so they can be deciphered again—is a painful, never-ending challenge for the 1 in 5 kids with dyslexia whose brain is wired differently.

Traditional approaches to reading that work for a sizeable majority of students just don't work for them.

Because they're not dumb, only different, reading hurts their feelings and their self-esteem when others make fun, as well as their ability to achieve academic success when they can't process everyday class work or do well on tests that don't measure their strengths.

Outside class, the student with dyslexia may be a bright, inquisitive kid with a great sense of humor and an easy-going way. He can take apart and rebuild a bicycle, refinish a vintage skateboard and see the seams on a fastball, making him a savvy power hitter on his baseball travel team. She can draw plants and animals, soar on the volleyball court. They are the ones who lead the way on a hike, spot the bird nest in a hedge, and the hawk high in the sky.

In speech and actions, these kids who struggle to read reveal a well-developed sense of fairness, empathy and self-reflection. They listen intently and pick up details, patterns and compassionate understanding of issues and situations in personal relationships.

But the classroom is another story altogether. Listening to students with dyslexia read out loud is nearly as painful for the listener, as it is for them, as they stumble, skip words, guess, and get lost on the page. Taking a spelling test is a revelation in improvisation, with little or no understanding of homonyms, silent letters, consonant-vowel blends or the basic sounds of letters in the English language. Their inability to crack the code of anomalies makes it virtually impossible for them to get a passing grade without lots of support.

Despite struggles with the written word, these students speak well—organizing deep thoughts that inform, and providing insightful conclusions that startle. They tell stories with rich descriptive details, using metaphor, analogy, leaps of imagination and empathic understanding.

Just don't ask them to write the story down. The connection between what's going on in their minds—and how to transcribe it using fingers—just isn't there. The result is a labored, almost indecipherable scrawl or letters so run together they may not even be able to read them later.

It can take a long time to discover that disconnect is actually dyslexia, which contributes to a wired-a-little-differently, right-brain-dominant, creative, intuitive, concrete thinker who sees the big picture, but has little patience for the details of academics that most children grasp in their journey through their school years.

What every parent needs to know is that for some bright and motivated students, school can be the source of great joy and for others—just as bright and motivated—a source of tremendous pain. The struggle creeps up unexpectedly, subtly at first, then more obviously, and finally unavoidably—presenting different challenges to the child in elementary, middle, and high school.

TRAVELING THROUGH THE GRADES

A combination of early identification, appropriate instruction delivered by experienced and well-trained educators, and proper classroom accommodations are of immeasurable help for students with dyslexia as they travel through the grades.

12

Elementary School

The formative years of primary school, from Kindergarten through sixth grade, lay the foundation of a child's educational experience and the development of important skills—in written and spoken language, as well as understanding mathematic concepts, and awareness of history and citizenship.

Fundamental to all of this and most essential, is learning to read write and spell. Without a strong foundation, academic success in elementary school—and beyond—is problematic, if not unlikely.

Teacher Training

Studies show that the most important factors in student success when it comes to reading are the knowledge and skills of the teacher. What happens to a child with dyslexia when the elementary school teacher is not well-schooled when it comes to recognizing dyslexia, and addressing it? How is that child going to learn how to read?

As is too often the case, teacher training in dyslexia is seriously lacking in our public schools system.

Also unfortunately, the child's early struggles with the written word may be initially attributed to normal immaturity, as a developmental delay, as an issue of motivation, or as a characteristic of ADD or ADHD. Dyslexia is typically the last word on the list, when it should be among the first, particularly if there is a history of dyslexia in the family. Parents who express their concern may be put off, literally for years, before assessments begin and, by that time, their child's skills are far behind those of their peers. These delays may lead to behavior and self-esteem issues.

Caring teachers may feel reluctant to voice a concern, and unwilling to make an assumption too early for fear of improperly "labeling" a young child. Or they may have district-imposed limitations on the number of students they refer for testing.

Learning about the early signs of dyslexia helps parents be more proactive about identifying—and communicating to the school staff—the child's strengths and weaknesses. Remember that "Wait to Fail" is the default operating system of most schools and school districts.

Early identification of students with dyslexia and proper intervention are optimal, providing much more time for different learners to own their differences and to master ways to compensate in the classroom. Several states take a proactive approach by mandating univer-sal screening of kindergarteners.

Making Progress

When I first realized my own son was having more trouble reading than his peers—long before he was ever tested or diagnosed—I looked for information at the educational store, the local bookshop and even the office supplies store. I bought flash cards, workbooks and all kinds of summer bridge and "what your child should know" type books to supplement his school-work. None of them helped him become a better reader.

Our regular visits to the bookstore were discouraging at best. He mastered Early Reader-stage books, but not much beyond that. As he got older, these books were much "too babyish," as he described it. He could not decipher the grade-level books—and above—that his friends were reading, and made it clear he didn't want me to read them aloud to him. Frustrated and embar-rassed, we left the shop empty-handed many times.

I remember asking the usually helpful clerk in the children's section where to find information about books that feature characters with learning differences or who have trouble reading. "Nothing on the shelves about that subject," she confessed with an apology. Many more resources on the subject of learning differences and dyslexia are now available: informative and entertaining books with memorable characters and inspirational role models. Progress!

Switching Schools

By the time my son completed second grade, it was obvious he was struggling, so I decided to take him out of his public "alternative school of choice" with its relaxed, child-centered pedagogy, and place him in a "more structured" neighborhood public school—in the hopes of improving his focus and providing a more academic environment.

From Day One of third grade at the new school, I dragged my miserable little boy to class. He barely brightened when he returned home, burdened with rote memorization tasks and bombarded with weekly spelling words. The demands of this new high-achieving campus just made his school struggles worse. His papers were marked up with angry red pencil; his name was written on the board (but he never knew why), and he was regularly kept inside during recess as a punishment for his lack of achievement in class.

After three terrible weeks of this daily torture, my motherly instincts to protect my child's emotional well-being superseded my worry over his education issues. It wasn't just that he missed his friends and the familiarity of the other school; the "more structured" school was clearly destroying his spirit inside school and ruining his confidence outside of it. "I can't do anything right," he cried. He was right, he couldn't, not in that environment. The tipping point was when a spelling test fell out of his backpack. A large red 2/20 was circled with the note: Capitals = Wrong!!!

I went back to the alternative school and begged to reclaim his place in the class. Thankfully, he was able to return to the school where he was appreciated for his strengths; where they emphasized collaborative, project-based learning, and no teacher would ever think of marking up a paper with a red pencil.

My thinking was that we would eventually figure out what to do about the reading issue, but a return to a nurturing environment would at least return him to his cheerful, enthusiastic self. A few weeks later, he brought home some school pictures that had been taken at the "more structured" school; I barely recognized the dispirited child who could not even smile for the camera, his grimace frozen for all time.

"Oh, honey, what are these?" I asked my son, who was back to his happy place in an environment that welcomed him and encouraged his talents. "You look so sad."

He smiled sweetly and said, "Mom, those are pictures they took of me at that school that was like a jail for kids."

It felt like a knife in my stomach. "I am so sorry I sent you there," I said, barely holding back hot tears.

"It's okay," he shrugged. "You're my mom, and you take care of me. But I'm happy to be at my real school again." He ran off to play, while I sat down and sobbed.

Again, he was right. I thought I did know what was best—structure, academics, more intensity. But I didn't have any assurances from the school, nor did I then possess enough specific knowledge to know what he needed. Lesson learned: Do your homework before making a major change in your child's education to make sure that the new approach really is significantly better than the old one. If it is, give thanks that you have access to a superior option, and make the change. If not, keep looking for another placement.

Retention

Research and anecdotal evidence indicate that having a child repeat a grade, held back and separated from peers, is a traumatic experience that is not likely to provide any notable educational benefit. The National Association of School Psychologists addressed the issue of retention in a policy statement, noting, "NASP urges educators to use methods other than grade retention and social promotion to ensure that all students have access to effective and equitable education."

Particularly for dyslexic students, simply exposing them to the same approach that didn't work the first time basically sets them up for failure the second time— and may establish a negative pattern for their rest of their lives. What does work are approaches designed o teach dyslexic students in the way they learn.

Elementary Education for Parents

Here is an Action Plan for Parents to help elementary school children with difficulties in reading, writing, spelling, and/or arithmetic. (Note: these tips are appropriate for older children, too, but our goal here is early identification and to get appropriate teaching methods instituted as soon as possible in a student's schooling.)

1) **Think back to your own academic history.** Ask if other family members had reading struggles. Some learning differences, including dyslexia, are hereditary. Often to their surprise, many parents identify their own dyslexia when in the position of figuring out what's happening with their struggling child.

2) **Learn about your school district's reading programs**. Insist that your child be taught reading in a structured, direct, evidence-based, multi-sensory approach (Orton-Gillingham) designed for students with dyslexia. It must be provided by a trained educator who delivers it with fidelity. Don't let anyone give you a computer-based reading program, or a program out of a box that's all about whole language or balanced literacy, instead of direct, explicitly instruction by an experienced educator.

3) **Plan to hire a tutor.** (or teach your child on your own). Make certain the professional is trained and skilled in

dealing with dyslexia. Students with dyslexia need a sequential, structured approach to reading instruction in order to be successful, and there is no time to waste working with someone without experience in tutoring with the Orton-Gillingham method.

4) **Beware of mis-identification**. Educators often confuse the characteristics of dyslexia in the classroom with ADD and ADHD. When dyslexic students are not engaged with the assignment or the lecture, their attention may wander, and they may gaze out the window, doodle, or tap a foot. Educators may interpret these behaviors as attention issues, rather than as indicators of dyslexia. But parents may be very aware that their dyslexic child can spend hours with complete focus on a favorite activity, like building a model or creating a painting. Be wary if an educator suggests medication based on classroom observation only.

5) **Find a support group (or start your own).** Network and educate yourself as much as possible about how to be a successful advocate, attend workshops, seminars, and find help online. Learn about nonprofits that are dedicated to serving the community of learning differences and seek out their information, resources and advocacy services if necessary. Consider joining local, national and even international organizations dedicated to supporting

the research, education and political lobbying efforts of the dyslexia community.

6) **Support your child's interests and strengths.** Many children with dyslexia have talent in music, drama, art, sports or science. Resist the urge to cut out those activities in order to focus on traditional academics. Your child needs these creative outlets, and your support shows you understand how they add meaning and success to a child who struggles daily in school.

7) **Provide role models.** Educate your child about his or her learning style, strengths and where support might be needed. Point out famous successful people with dyslexia, and share the many age-appropriate books for children with dyslexia.

8) **Remember that reading and spelling skills do not equal intelligence**. In the early years, it's so difficult to remember that simple fact. Make certain your child is not defined by his or her ability to read or spell. Early struggles must not define a child's emotional wellbeing or sense of confidence. Be alert for any bullying your child may experience in the classroom, the playground or the neighborhood. It can sound something like: "Well, maybe I can't play baseball as good as you, but at least I'm smart enough to read, not like you, dumb-head."

Hitting the Third Grade Wall

Third grade is one of the most important years of a student's life. It is the crucial year that's all about reading mastery or falling behind. The correlation between third grade reading levels and future success is profound: students who can't read at grade level in third grade are four times less likely to graduate from high school than their peers who can.

Third grade marks the difference between learning to read and reading to learn; the end of reading text accompanied by illustrations and photos that provide clues that help struggling students slide through school without actually reading.

A perfect example is the very bright dyslexic student who had spent his summer in Wisconsin, where he had the opportunity to witness a colony of beavers building a dam. When he went back to school, as a new 4th grader, the reading assignment was about a beaver dam; he volunteered to "read" out loud, and told a wonderful story about all that activity he had keenly observed; it had, of course, no correlation to the paragraphs on the page. The teacher was completely baffled by his "reading" until the mom let her know where he'd gained all his knowledge about beavers—a long way from the classroom, and that particular book.

His workaround technique of picking up context from pictures and using acquired knowledge had finally caught up with him, and now he had to learn how to read. When he was finally assessed, he was already three years behind his peers, and his parents had to embark on a years-long quest to build and remediate his approach to reading. Now a student in middle school, he's catching up, after considerable private instruction, and intensive summer sessions with an Orton-Gillingham trained tutor. He was one of the lucky ones.

A more common story is for the child to continue to struggle after third grade, and well into middle school, where the window for reading instruction rapidly closes.

Considering Special Education

During the elementary school years, parents need to consider Special Education for their child. Special Ed is where dyslexia services are typically delivered and if parents want these services for their child, they need to learn what they can get, and from whom.

After comprehensive testing of a student for all suspected disabilities is completed, the parents will be invited to a meeting to determine eligibility for Special Education services. During this initial meeting, an educational psychologist will go over the battery of tests in detail—what some consider mind-numbing detail. If your child is deemed eligible for services, a document called an IEP—Individualized Education Program—will be drafted.

The details required for hammering out an acceptable IEP are really a book of their own. Indeed, many books have been written on the subject, and multiple advocates and attorneys specialize in dealing with the legal aspects of them. (Learn more at wrightslaw.com and refer to the "Dyslexia and Special Education" chapter in this book.)

Five IEP Tips for Parents

1) Understand your rights before attending any IEP meeting.

2) Keep your cool and be polite; always remember to consider the needs of your child.

3) Make certain you understand all provisions of an IEP before you sign it—do NOT sign it at the IEP meeting, but take time to review it and the notes that are taken during the meeting.

4) Bring a support person or advocate to take notes and to help clarify anything that is unclear.

5) The document is the last and only word. If it's not written in the IEP, it doesn't exist.

Hold teachers and administrators accountable for implementing the IEP that the entire team has worked so hard to craft. Ignore uninformed comments or insinuations from other parents that your child is getting something special or undeserved.

Standardized Testing and Students with Dyslexia

Standardized testing of American schoolchildren is the law of the land: It influences the way public schools receive funding and can even dictate whether or not teachers and administrators keep their jobs. High-stakes testing, indeed.

The annual ordeal is stressful enough for students who perform well on tests. For those with dyslexia, standardized testing can be a miserable experience with little or no positive payoff—and much opportunity for failure and incompetence.

"All that test prep and taking all those tests makes children better test-takers, so they should take every one they have a chance to take," argue some.

Others disagree with that testing-is-good-for-you approach. Knowing the risk-reward for standardized tests, and the very predictable results, parents of students with dyslexia may choose to exempt their children from these tests.

My son was tested, assessed and examined repeatedly in order to qualify for Special Education. Once he became so exasperated he balked and refused to take any more. In that vividly descriptive dyslexic fashion, he exclaimed: "I feel like a piece of meat that they're trying to tenderize, but I'm already burning on the barbecue."

We heard his protest, and told the district officials that he would not be subjected to more evaluations.

Educators agreed to an off-the-record approach: every year they formally suggested he take the tests, and every year we updated the letter stating our son would not be taking the battery of state-mandated standardized tests. Instead, he and his dad went camping during testing week. Undoubtedly father-son time spent in the great outdoors was more beneficial than day after day stuck in class filling in bubbles on a ScanTron.

Transition from Elementary to Middle School

Parents must stay involved to keep their children on track in school and in life outside the classroom, particularly during the early teen years. If your child has an IEP, be sure a meeting is scheduled to help make transitional plans for the big step up to middle school.

If your child does not qualify for Special Education services (or you choose not to get involved in Special Education), and does not have an IEP, you still need to get involved, possibly in the development of a 504 plan that will allow accommodations.

Elementary School to Middle School Transition To-Do List

✳ In the springtime before entering middle school, meet with academic counselors or administrators from the new school to communicate your child's needs and to learn about expectations and services.

✳ Schedule a meeting with your child's teachers early in the school year to clarify any issues of concern. That personal connection—better than a phone call or string of e-mails—will greatly help you in creating a team of support, and setting the stage for success, for your child.

✳ Some schools offer a variation on an "Individualized Instruction" (II) class, which may provide the opportunity to get help during a regularly scheduled class period. This extra support can be beneficial because the II teacher can communicate with other teachers and make sure the student is staying on track.

✳ Accommodations may include shortened homework assignments, assistive technology (audio books, note-taking assistance, software to organize writing, speech to text and text to speech, etc.), extra time on tests, preferential seating, a weekly check-in between parents and teachers, and alternative means of assessment such as verbal exams and projects, rather than written work to demonstrate mastery of material.

13

Middle School

Middle school is often the time when students with dyslexia can't fake it anymore. It's understandable as the "Learning to Read" days of the early primary grades give way to the "Reading to Learn" expectations. While some students with dyslexia may be able to keep up, barely hanging on through the end of elementary school, whatever coping mechanisms and workarounds got them through grades 5 or 6 are inadequate for middle school.

"I was dyslexic. I had no understanding of school-work whatsoever," declared Sir Richard Branson, billionaire entrepreneur, founder of Virgin Enterprises and the nonprofit organization Made by Dyslexia. "I certainly would have failed IQ tests. And it was one of the reasons I left school when I was 15 years old. And if I'm not interested in something, I don't grasp it."

The stresses of reading difficulties combined with the increased demands of staying organized for multiple classes and teachers, changing classes, using a locker and an ever-increasing load of homework can overwhelm the young adolescent. Add in the hormonal effects of their early teen years, and a desire to fit in with peers at all costs—and it's a recipe for disaster for the unidentified or under-accommodated middle-schooler with dyslexia.

This is also the time when students have more free-dom to make choices—including bad ones—that may lead them astray. Access to drugs and alcohol, and a larger population of peers who might have their own behavioral or socio-emotional issues can negatively affect even the most stable of students.

Middle School Challenges

The relentless pace of homework assignments, con-stant assessments, increased need for reading difficult textbook assignments under tight time constraints, as well as coping with the requirements of multiple teach-ers—determined to create "rigor" in their classes and to develop "grit" in their students—add to the stress and struggles of students with (and without) dyslexia.

Alienation from the classroom, escape into depres-sion and withdrawal from authority figures are common occurrences, at a time when teens want more indepen-dence and less help from their parents than ever before.

The downward emotional and academic spiral associated with students who struggle with dyslexia is likely to occur in middle school. Parents and teachers must be on guard with this age group, and prepared to intervene and assist immediately.

Two challenges in particular must be addressed. Middle-schoolers are expected to be well-organized and punctual. Executive function issues typically accompany dyslexia and compound academic challenges. They are also typically expected to study a foreign language—even if they can barely master the complexities of English.

If your child's reading level continues to be problematic, insist that the school provide appropriate instruction, remediation, and support—not just accommodations for low skill levels.

Make sure your child enrolls in enjoyable elective classes; these are a welcome daily break from the high-demand academic ones. Resist at all costs the negative and punitive solutions of taking away an art class or other "fun" class in favor of two math or two English classes—which will overwhelm the student even more. Creativity and fun are essential components of a well-rounded education.

Support your child's strengths and creative interests in and outside of school by encouraging extra-curricular activities, including athletics, drama, dance, music, robot-building—whatever provides a sense of pride, and feeling of accomplishment.

Middle School to High School Transition To-Do List

✳ Parents must continue to be proactive in helping dyslexic teens along the trail from middle school to high school. Of all the public school experiences, high school can be the one fraught with potential for difficulty. Stakes are higher, the potential for "failure" greater, and the opportunities for misunderstandings—and getting lost in the shuffle—are magnified with multiple teachers.

✳ In the spring of your child's last year of middle school, schedule a transition meeting with school officials—and invite a representative from the high school to attend. By involving a member from the high school at this early stage and providing as much information as possible about your child's learning style, need for accommodations, personality preferences, and, especially strengths and interests, you'll increase the chances for a successful transition. At the very least, you will have provided an introduction to a familiar face on an unfamiliar campus.

automatically occurs in it

✳ Encourage your child to visit the high school campus in advance to become familiar with its layout; to learn from older friends what classes and teachers might be particularly good matches, and to be confident about striding onto that campus with every expectation for success.

✳ If an Individualized Instruction class is recommended, and supposed to be a time when the student receives Special Education services, you need to determine that there really is instruction, and it's not just a study hall or a free-for-all when everyone is chatting, dozing, or playing on their phones.

✳ Make sure that your student has at least one freshman class that is an elective of interest to relieve the grind of required academics

✳ Create a one- to two-page document about your child's educational experiences, learning style, strengths and weakness, accommodations and other pertinent information that will help high school educators become familiar with your child's classroom needs. Few classroom teachers will read—much less fully understand—a multi-page IEP, so creating something like an Executive Summary can really help. School officials themselves may take the time to create a document something like this, called "Fast Facts" or other catchy phrase. Other strategies by parents include making a single sheet for their child to keep in their notebook or making a short video. One very proactive mother created a website about her son so that teachers could refer to it!

Sample Memo from Parents
Re: Transition from Middle School to High School

Background

1) Our son's challenges with dyslexia were not fully identified and addressed until he was in seventh grade, still reading at a second-grade level. At that time, he received intensive, one-on-one remedial reading instruction. He worked very hard and is now able to read at grade level.

2) While there has been a vast improvement in his reading skills and comprehension, his spelling and handwriting skills remain many grade levels behind and will continue to lag far behind his college-level vocabulary and oral presentation abilities.

3) He also had unaddressed challenges in math. In eighth grade, he received intensive, one-on-one instruction in math, and now has achieved competency and confidence in his understanding and abilities.

4) His challenges include time-management, reading aloud, organization, memorization and quick recall of facts, test-taking, spelling, and handwriting.

Strengths to support

5) He thinks in pictures, and is a hands-on, auditory, and kinesthetic learner who is best engaged in collaborative group activities.

6) His strengths include frequent and meaningful contributions to classroom discussions, dictating essays that are impactful and show a high degree of reasoning and elevated vocabulary, oral and mixed-media presentations.

7) He is a gifted athlete, one of the very best baseball players in his age group in the area.

8) He has always been respected and admired by his teachers and fellow students for his optimism, calm demeanor, work ethic, emotional maturity, problem-solving abilities and leadership skills.

Challenges to address

Like many, he is easily embarrassed about his dyslexia and related challenges that make him "different" from others. He is all too aware that the popular perception is "dyslexia = dumb." And, regrettably, "Special Ed" is still a stigma, one that affects him.

Although there has been much emphasis on his gifts (leadership, innate intelligence, perceptions of detail, 3-D thinking, etc.), his weaknesses in a traditional school setting have the potential to affect him not only in academics, but to undermine his sense of confidence and competence in other areas of life. This is an area of primary concern.

14

Dyslexia High

J ust when you might think it's time you can relax and send your bigger-than-you-ever-imagined young adult off to the high-school campus, you may find that dyslexia is not recognized there.

This is no time to take a break. Realize that even though our high school sons and daughters may want desperately to be independent, they still need our help in so many ways. This especially applies to those high-schoolers with dyslexia.

Parents of high school students must get involved from the get-go and push for proper accommodations, or their high-schoolers with learning differences will get lost.

Or worse—much worse—is the possibility of doing drugs, dropping out, acting out in myriad destructive ways—leading to trouble with the juvenile justice system and worst of all, self-harm or suicide for those who see no end in sight to the misery they experience.

Get Involved and Stay Involved

Be proactive in every way you can, but also be prepared—and prepare your teen—for the unexpected. Early in my son's freshman year, I got so exasperated with the multiplying effect of his negative experiences, that I created a new mantra for myself. "I don't care anymore what you teach him, just don't hurt him." I said it to more than one teacher and administrator at the school and at the district level, particularly after a series of preventable situations occurred that resulted in a downward emotional and academic spiral.

After just seven days in high school, my son came to me and said, "I have 173 more days of this. I can't do it, Mom. I just can't."

It turned out that during his first week of school, my son's carefully crafted IEP filled with appropriate accommodations hadn't been distributed to any of his teachers. School policy was not to distribute them until the third week of school! *Do you know how much failure and humiliation a dyslexic student can endure in the first three weeks of school?*

In those first weeks, my son was repeatedly asked to read aloud (when the IEP did not allow it), was overloaded with in-class reading and writing assignments, felt overwhelmed by pop quizzes, and was totally unable to take notes from the board. While tops in the class at using tools, he was even failing woodshop because he couldn't pass the *written* safety exam.

No wonder he totaled up the number of days ahead as though it was a jail sentence!

When I asked the Special Education director at the high school why there wasn't better communication and understanding between Special Education and General Education, she just sighed heavily, and said, "That's the way it's always been, and that's the way it always will be."

Well, she was wrong about that. Thankfully, a new principal, John Becchio, had just arrived, one who listened and learned. We began to work collaboratively to solve some of these painful issues. Our strategies included picking teachers who were most receptive to the needs of dyslexic students, and scheduling face-to-face meetings with all those teachers at the beginning of the year. His leadership, and willingness to work together, made a huge difference. Over time, we figured out ways to help not just my son, but other different learners like him, and changed the school culture in doing so.

All this took place at Santa Barbara High School, the same high school that notable dyslexia advocate Charles Schwab attended, Class of 1955—exactly 60 years before my son's graduation in 2015.

In most cases, however, the size of a typical American public high school—and the lean budgets so common these days—creates conditions that are difficult for students with dyslexia. Too many students are in a classroom and overburdened teachers may not have the training or skills needed to provide differentiated or specialized instruction. There is little to no reading instruction or appropriate remediation, and teachers and administrators are unwilling or resistant to implementing accommodations.

Add to that the common misunderstandings about the characteristics of dyslexia—which may include time management, organizational issues and difficulty taking notes from lectures—and the student with dyslexia is at a significant disadvantage compared to others. It's no wonder that the dropout rate of students with dyslexia is twice that of other students.

Be Prepared

Expect the unexpected: Scan-Trons for testing (frequently difficult for students with dyslexia to keep straight); the combination locker that is too confusing for a student with dyslexia to use (try a keyed locker instead); the teacher who decides accommodations are unnecessary on a test; homework assignments that are corrected in class by peers (resulting in much embarrassment); the never-ending issue of reading aloud in class; the coach who bellows, "What's the matter with you, are you dyslexic?"

Be prepared for the additional pressures of non-dyslexic friends who take more prestigious (and more academically challenging and rewarding) Honors or Advanced Placement classes, or enroll in exclusive academies or "schools within a school," while your equally bright child is stuck in what's generously called "College Prep" these days.

Increasingly, these College Prep classes are low-level classes characterized by a disconnected circular pattern between teacher and student, with teachers who have low expectations, and students who become checked out and unmotivated. It's impossible to know how much of this is caused by unidentified learning differences, but whatever the cause, it is pervasive.

Students with dyslexia can succeed in challenging and innovative classes, especially those that emphasize project-based learning and accumulating portfolios, but due to the amount of reading, homework, and testing typically required, they are often discouraged from enrolling in them.

Add in the expectation for self-advocacy (even though they never seem to be taught exactly *how* to self-advocate, or anything at all about the characteristics of their learning difference) and it's obvious that the traditional high school structure creates great difficulties for students who learn differently.

When Administrators and Teachers Just Don't Get Dyslexia

During an IEP meeting for a high school sophomore, an educational psychologist—with the principal of the school seated right at the table—stated: "These kids with learning disabilities just need to learn how to suck it up." A high school junior and his parents were at an IEP meeting when one of his general education teachers, turned on her student and burst out: "You never smile in class, and I don't know what to do with you."

Parents have many more stories like this to share when they ask for help when their kids are falling apart. The stories parents tell of time wasted and blame placed on these teens who just don't fit in the regular classroom are sad beyond belief.

A pro basketball coach recently gave his team an F-(minus) for its off-season actions. Then he mused about whether or not there's such a thing as an F-. Well, yes there is. In high school.

In a freshman health class my son was given a grade of F- on a test because his teacher didn't allow him to use his accommodations. She claimed that she knew he was smart, and didn't think that he needed them. Then she told him she thought that a little extra pressure was good for him.

What made matters even worse is that she then had students trade papers for grading, and when the cute girl next to him marked his paper all wrong, he was as mortified as he's ever been. The experience set him on a downhill spiral that took a few weeks and a spring term vacation to get back his confidence and sense of well-being.

When I talked with the teacher about it, she kept telling me, "Don't you think that giving him accommodations is just coddling him? I mean, what will he do when he gets into the real world?"

The good news is that I talked with the assistant principal and the principal about this terrible episode, and they agreed to adjust the computers to eliminate the possibility of an F- grade for any student. Four years later, my son graduated from high school with honors and his self-esteem restored. But I'll bet he will never forget the humiliation he felt from that incident with a teacher who just didn't get it, but thought she did.

There was a bright spot in the form of geometry teacher, Jenn Fastman, who sent this note at the end of the school year: *I really enjoyed having Daniel in class this year; he really is a great kid. Also, I appreciated learning a lot about children with dyslexia this year and it's helped me help other students with dyslexia as well, so I would like to thank you for opening my eyes up to this world.*

Remediation or Accommodation?

Because my son learned to read before high school, he was somewhat ready for the challenges when he arrived for his freshman year. At least he had been taught the skills he needed to read at grade level—not fast, and not enjoyably, but with the ability to do so. And because he attended an alternative-type elementary and middle school that focused on "the whole child," his curiosity and self-esteem were intact as well.

However, many dyslexic students have challenging elementary school and middle school experiences, and are never taught in the way they learn. They get passed along, from grade to grade with their dyslexia never identified, and never taught how to read past a third-grade level.

By the time they reach high school, there is no going back: high schools rarely provide remedial programs in reading and math for these students to catch up. They are simply expected to figure it out. If the student has an IEP, modest goals are stated and limited accommodations written, but no longer is there a way for them to receive the kind of basic instruction they need.

Suddenly, and unexpectedly, students with learning differences are blamed for their missing skill set, and when they act out, zone out, or just skip school altogether, they may slide into the world of never-ending disapproval, consequences, and even the juvenile justice system, sometimes called the "school to prison pipeline."

Exit Exams and Other Requirements

Some states require students to demonstrate their proficiency in reading, writing and math in order to receive their high school diploma. Early in your teen's high school career, check with appropriate administrators about how to obtain accommodations for these tests. If your school district requires a student to take and fail the tests before a waiver can be offered—in my view an unnecessary exercise in futility—do the best you can to help your student prepare, and minimize, the emotional damage if that happens.

Many districts may require the completion of community service hours before graduation. Strive to make this experience meaningful for your high school student, and help find a volunteer experience that will support strengths and interests. There are many ways to maximize success, and it all starts with building relationships with personnel at the school. Do all you can to communicate and collaborate with school officials, including the Special Education director, your child's case manager, principal, teachers, counselors, coaches and to develop ways to eliminate obstacles to your child's success.

College Testing

Students who have an IEP or 504 for a documented learning difference typically qualify for accommodations for the PSAT and SAT, as well as on the Advanced Placement tests. During your teen's freshman year, communicate with the school counselor and/or the Special Education director about applying for appropriate accommodations through the College Board Services for Students with Disabilities. Typical accommodations include scribes for written responses, extra time and alternate settings. Accommodations are also available for the ACT through its Services for Students with Disabilities.

Remember that high school, while it may seem like forever, is a short-term proposition, and there is plenty of life beyond it. Students with dyslexia can excel in college and should be encouraged to pursue higher education. However, students with dyslexia who have entrepreneurial ambitions or who prefer hands-on trades may reasonably decide to choose other directions after high school.

When he applied for admission to colleges, my son Daniel decided to write about his struggle with dyslexia in his Common Application Essay.

Ten Strategies for High School Success

1) **Arrange face-to-face meetings** with as many general education teachers as possible at the beginning of the school year to provide insights and explain your child's learning style, strengths and weaknesses, and how best to communicate any problems or issues that may come up during the school year.

2) **Plan your child's schedule carefully** and seek the input of others to determine the best classes/teachers who will work cooperatively with you to educate your child. Work to develop a schedule that allows much-needed "down time," usually elective classes in an area of interest, and without much homework or additional stress.

3) **Realize teacher limitations.** Not every teacher has the awareness, willingness or ability to successfully implement necessary accommodations and modifications. Be patient, and share resources when possible. Treat all teachers with respect, and you may be able to change hearts and minds, and encourage more understanding.

4) **Go where the love is.** Figure out positive work-arounds to help your teen accomplish goals with successful strategies whenever possible. For example, foreign language requirements can often trip up college-bound dyslexic students, subjecting them to unnecessary stress; consider acceptable options like American Sign Language, cultural studies or even computer coding classes instead. These classes may be taken online or at the local community college if they are not offered through the school district or on the high school campus.

5) **Develop a strong and enforceable IEP or 504 Plan.** Insist on appropriate accommodations that will allow your teen to be successful in the daily classroom experience—and in assessments of knowledge gained.

6) **Help with homework.** Plan to spend several hours with your teen going over homework assignments, helping with organizational tasks; perhaps even helping out as a scribe for writing assignments, or reading aloud, if needed. If there's a You Tube explanation or

a movie available to enrich and enhance an assignment, help find it and use it as a visual supplement. Ask your teen to inquire about how to obtain extra credit—particularly in an area of their greatest strengths—to provide extra points and an alternative means of assessment in case there's a "bombed" test or assignment.

7) **Participate in other school activities.** In addition to dealing with your teen's learning differences, attend sporting events, plays and musical performances and contribute your time, talent, and financial support as best you can.

8) **Support your teen's strengths.** Remember that participation in these extra-curricular activities, whether they're in the arts, athletics, science, film-making, writing poetry, whatever, is what makes school worth attending for many, many students who can hardly wait for the final bell to ring each day.

9) **About athletics:** If your teen is an athlete who must maintain academic eligibility in order to play, you must stay on top of the graded assignments and exams. Monitor the grades weekly, and ask to be notified if your teen's grades ever drop below a C. The worst possible development for an aspiring student-athlete who feels free on the field of play is to get benched for academic reasons. (Of course, if the IEP or 504 is working, the student should *never* fail.)

10) **Teach your teen self-advocacy skills.** Provide information about successful role models who have dyslexia; discuss characteristics of your teen's learning style and encourage ownership of the differences—and communication about it. Make understanding this learning difference simply a matter-of-fact part of life as much as possible.

Reflections: Graduation Day

As more than 500 students filed into the football stadium, my eyes were fixed on just one—my brave, hardworking and smart son who had worked so hard to fulfill all the requirements to earn his high school diploma. It was the culmination of a 13-year journey that began with a hug from his kindergarten teacher greeting him with, "Hello, sunshine!" to a firm handshake from a school board member who said, "Congratulations, young man."

So much that was said and done in the time in between those memorable moments.

I felt such a sense of pride, mixed with relief and joy, watching my son walk across the stage as his name was called, knowing what a long, hard and soul-wearying trip it had been through DyslexiaLand. But he earned his credits, completed every requirement and always did his best, no matter how difficult the task.

Along with his cap and gown, he wore the golden cords signifying his membership in the National Honor Society and his achievements in the classroom and beyond. He beamed as he transferred the tassel from one side to the other, and shouted with joy when he threw the mortarboard into the air. Finally released from the public school classroom, he was free to chart his own course into the future.

Although he had been accepted at a fine private college, and awarded a generous scholarship, he chose to take a well-deserved gap year to put space between academics and real-life learning—and more importantly, give himself some time to process his options.

As his long-time advocate, I too, felt a great deal of relief with his high school graduation. No more making a case for a proper public education to educators; no more convoluted IEP goals to achieve; no more late-night worries about what might happen to my son if he couldn't jump through every hoop tossed his way. I had spent so much time working to keep his spirit intact while trying to increase the understanding of dyslexia among his educators, administrators, decision-makers and politicians.

Such a long journey; what an education we had all received. A weight felt lifted from my shoulders, as it was time, finally, to celebrate.

"We did it, Mom!" he said as he hugged me after I found him on the field, crowded with fellow students and their families. All the struggles of this part of his life were over, with a great new journey awaiting him, to make all the difference in the world.

Afterword

Each of us arrives in DyslexiaLand with a different set of experiences, different perspectives on politics, religion, and child-rearing but there is one overriding issue that unites us above all else: the desire and determination to do our best to help our children with dyslexia.

Once you know about dyslexia, it's almost impossible to keep quiet about it! We who work so hard to help our dyslexic children get through school have such a strong sense of connection with others who do the same; we can strike up a conversation with a perfect stranger—who immediately feels like a friend—and talk for hours about it. Oh, how it helps to tell our stories and listen to others tell theirs, knowing we are not alone, and neither are our children.

We share our triumphs and compare our troubles, seeking safety, justice and a sense of peace that we're on the right path as we make the long journey through DyslexiaLand. Along the way, no matter what our actual professions or areas of expertise, we develop new skills as we are called on to become advocates, assistive technology experts, behavioral professionals; book buyers, cheerleaders, community leaders, correspondents, counselors, curriculum specialists, detectives, diplomats, document and systems analysts, educational consultants, fact-checkers, financial managers, fund-raisers, grant-writers, homework helpers, legal-eagles, lobbyists, negotiators, peacemakers, persuasive speakers, political commentators, record-keepers, researchers, schedulers, social media mavens, socio-emotional assessors, teachers, test evaluators; tutors—and sometimes we're magicians, motivators and miracle workers.

All the while doing our best to keep clear heads, kind hearts, cheerful spirits and a sense of serenity as we raise happy, healthy families; maintain relationships outside the home and in the community, and hold onto our sanity and our jobs—even when we have to take too much time off to advocate for our children during school hours. Even when we have to keep our emotions in check and our opinions to ourselves—at least until we get home and let it all out in our safe place.

We take on these roles, develop our skills and work tirelessly to benefit the most precious people in our lives—our children, who depend on us to provide and care for them. Keep this purpose in mind at all times to prevent getting lost in DyslexiaLand. It's not about us; it's about creating more dyslexia-friendly experiences in our schools and communities and beyond.

And it's about the 1 in 5 children who have an extraordinarily different way of learning, thinking and embracing this big, beautiful world just waiting for them to reach their full potential so they can make their mark on it.

Acknowledgements

I am grateful for the generous and consistent support from Brynn Crowe, who has supported my advocacy efforts on behalf of children with dyslexia and their parents, and helped lead the way toward a greater community-wide understanding of dyslexia in Santa Barbara. Another resonating thank you goes to the Kirby-Jones Family Foundation.

I appreciate the wise counsel from friends and healers Kathleen Boisen and Gloria Menedes; and from stellar teachers and great neighbors Susan Petty and Julie Wood; longtime supportive friends Jane Fleischman, Milton Love, Nadya Penoff, Loretta Redd, Helene Webb, Denise Spooner, Penny and Terry Davies, Mike and Vivian Pahos, daughter Sophia Rose, sister Cindy, and real-life fairy godmother, Fotine O'Connor.

It's been my privilege to share the stories of Harvey Hubbell V, John Rodrigues, Victor Villasenor; and to work with Dr. John Becchio, former principal of Santa Barbara High School; Dr. Ben Drati, superintendent of Santa Monica-Malibu school district; Stephen and Jennifer Polk of Identifying.org; Dr. David Cash, former superintendent of Santa Barbara Unified School District.

Many thanks to Open Alternative School teachers Nitin Anand, David Archer, Marilyn Lauer, Brian Malcheski, Ann Silva and Alex Tashma. And a warm shout-out to Santa Barbara High School teachers Eric Nichoson and Jenn Fastman, and Lindamood-Bell's Janelle Ashby, Dana Ellingson and Mary Lyman.

Thanks also to County Supervisor Das Williams for his steadfast support and co-sponsorship of AB 1369 when he served in the state Assembly; current Assembly Member Monique Limon and former City Council Member Michael

Self for their understanding and support; to Joan and Les Esposito, who blazed the dyslexia trail for many years with their Dyslexia Awareness and Resource Center, and to Hod and Laraine Gray, of the Special Needs Project.

In my local community, a big thank you goes to Ed Heron, who offered his support on the school board and off; Christine Feldman, Paul Zink, and Joe Chenoweth, the best dyslexia panelists anywhere; Elvia Hernandez and Michelle Meyering of the Police Activities League; Dayton Aldrich and Adam Howland of the Santa Barbara District Attorney's Office; Bev Schwartzberg and Jody Thomas at the Santa Barbara Public Library; Monie DeWit for her creative spark, and a host of community angels who tirelessly work with students with dyslexia, including Anna Bisker, Pam Boswell, Jessica Bowman, Michele Britton Bass, Deidre and Barry Dubin, Jana Garnett, Pat Johnson, Kerry Katch, Linda Locker, Kristin Sethre, Jane Swain, Helaina Takeda and so many more.

Dyslexia Warrior Moms from across California and around the nation were unflagging with their inspirational comments and support. Thank you so much Lisa Baye Kaye, Jennifer Sheri Biang, Faith Borkowsky, Stacey Bower Cavaglieri, Tandy Camberg Harris, Pamela Cohen, Tina Marie DeLong, Amy Dingillo-Tompkins, Lorraine Donovan, Colleen Fournier, Tracy Gillette; Theresa Graham, Irene Granados Tackett, Lois Holguin, Rachel Hurd, Clarice Jackson, Lisa Klipfel, Haya Kohn Sakadjian, Rose Kuntz, Jm Lawrence, Lisa Lloyd Riggs, Deborah Lynam, Kari Marshall Cone, Katie McCustion, Lisa Nelson, Jean Pasternak, Tobie Piowaty-Palmer Meyer, Judith Reising, Sherrry Rubacalva, Rosette Schleifer Roth, Stephanie Setmire, Peggy Stern, Jamie Stone, Lori Stone DePole, Caron Trout, Enid Webb, and many more.

I have been honored to support hundreds of families in their travels through DyslexiaLand, and have profound gratitude for those who shared their stories and experiences in order to help others along the way.

About the Artist

Liz Taylor is an illustrator, cartoonist and storyteller. Her work brings a smile, and sometimes a tear, by telling stories through whimsical pictures and characters. Much of her work explores the challenges children face in school: feeling overlooked and misunderstood, overcoming learning disabilities and social issues like friendship difficulties. She often communicates her ideas about school experiences through the tools children use to learn, like books and school supplies.

As the parent of a dyslexic child, Liz lent her artistic talents to support the campaign that promoted passage of the first dyslexia law the State of Arizona in 2015. Her illustration, A Day in the Life of a Courageous Dyslexic Student, received national recognition by the advocacy groups Bright Solutions for Dyslexia and The Dyslexic Advantage.

Liz resides in Phoenix, AZ with her husband and two neurologically diverse children. Her work can be found on Instagram at @liztaylorcreative or at liztaylorcreative.com.

1 in 5: The Face of Dyslexia

1 in 5: The Face of Dyslexia is an photographic awareness campaign about dyslexia, a fact of life for 1 in 5 individuals who attend school, work, play and contribute to every community. It features, in words and images, the range of talents, interests, perspectives and backgrounds of individuals with dyslexia. They share their stories and face the world with the goal of helping to create more dyslexia-friendly communities across the nation.

Presented online and exhibited in galleries, 1 in 5: The Face of Dyslexia is designed, produced and curated by mothers of children with dyslexia, author Cheri Rae and photographer Monie de Wit.

Learn more about this innovative campaign and view the gallery at DyslexiaLand.com

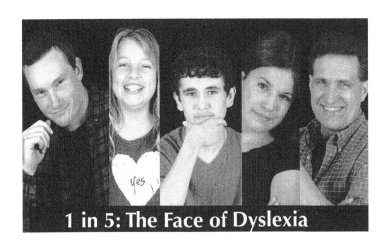

1 in 5: The Face of Dyslexia

About the Author

Two words best describe the direction of Cheri Rae's writing career: worthy causes. After graduating from California State University Northridge with a degree in Political Science, Cheri embarked on a path of good works that blended her desire to make a difference and her considerable editorial skills.

DyslexiaLand is a collection of hard-won wisdom gained over the course of ten years of advocacy for children with dyslexia, beginning with her own son. While serving as a consultant to the Santa Barbara Unified School District, Cheri established a Parent Resource Center, monthly "Dyslexia Dialogues" and a "Distinguished Dyslexic Speaker Series." She was named a "Local Hero" by the Santa Barbara Independent for her fearless efforts on behalf of students with dyslexia, and awarded a Resolution from the California State Assembly for her dyslexia work.

Prior to moving to Santa Barbara, Cheri enjoyed successful stints as a magazine editor, holding key management positions with such popular lifestyle magazines as *Runner's World, Surfer, California Scenic,* and *Bicycle Sport.* Cheri took up the cause of desert conservation and her maps and books, including *Mojave National Preserve: A Visitors Guide*, helped rally the public and contributed to a successful campaign that preserved the scenic wonders of the Mojave as national parkland.

In Santa Barbara, Cheri covered the city's lively political scene as a columnist for *Santa Barbara Daily Sound.* In 2009 the California Association of Newspaper Publishers, awarded Cheri first-place honors in the Best Newspaper Column category. Her interest in preserving—and celebrating—Santa Barbara's unique environment and architecture, led her to pen books about her fair city, including *Walk Santa Barbara: City Strolls & Country Rambles* and *Pearl Chase: First Lady of Santa Barbara.*

Cheri continues to work with parents leading parent empowerment seminars to help them advocate for their dyslexic children, writes articles, and shares the trials and tribulations of DyslexiaLand as a public speaker. Her dyslexia-related assemblage art has been featured in several galleries.

Cheri lives with her family in a 1912 bungalow in Santa Barbara's Bungalow Haven, located in the midst of the historic neighborhood district that she helped create through her advocacy. Learn more at DyslexiaLand.com.

Discover More About Dyslexia at
DYSLEXIALAND.COM

Made in the USA
Coppell, TX
22 July 2020

31525902R00154